"The FOCUSed15 Bible studies are for everyone
seem to get started. Chris and Katie Orr take th
and places a life-giving tool in your hand."
　　　　　　　　　　　　　　　　—ST,
　　　　　　　　　　　　　　　　　　　　　　　　　　.ˌ Jesus Worth It?

"Chris and Katie Orr have designed devotional material that leads the reader to encounter
the biblical text with guidance that reinforces solid principles of biblical interpretation and
helpful application that makes God's Word come alive in our daily choices."

—**TREVIN WAX**, Bible and Reference Publisher for LifeWay,
author, and general editor of *The Gospel Project*

"An ever-present need exists for a family-based, yet challenging study of the Bible. Chris
and Katie Orr have provided such a work. Their investigation into the Book of Philippians offers a diverse look into Scripture that is appropriate for personal study, couples'
devotions, or group Bible study. The material is biblically solid, with excellent exegetical
tools and application methods. Whether you are a new Christian or a seasoned follower of
Christ, this study will stimulate and encourage your faith."

—**WILLIAM D. HENARD,** DMin, PhD, LLD, executive director-treasurer,
West Virginia Convention of Southern Baptists

"Men and women are searching for discipleship tools for both themselves or others they
are discipling. Chris and Katie Orr have delivered up a fresh, substantive tool to accomplish
both. FOCUSed15 is a serious study method that is possible even for those with demanding responsibilities. This material will fit in a variety of settings for men and women everywhere on their spiritual journey."

—**DR. ED LITTON**, pastor of Redemption Church, Mobile, AL, and
KATHY LITTON, national consultant for ministry to pastors' wives,
North American Mission Board

"Chris and Katie Orr have a passion for Scripture and for men and women to know Scripture. This passion shows in their FOCUSed15 Bible study method, which they use to lead
others through books of the Bible and topical doctrinal studies. They prove that inductive
Bible study doesn't have to be complicated but can be deeply impactful and fruitful."

—**CHRISTINE HOOVER**, author of *Searching for Spring* and *Messy Beautiful Friendship*

"The FOCUSed15 Bible studies provide an opportunity to learn the tools of inductive Bible
study in bite-size chunks. Perfect for anyone who is committed to studying the Word in this
time-crunched culture!"

—**ANDREA BUCZYNSKI**, vice president, global leadership development/HR, Cru

"Chris and Katie Orr have brought a unique and productive method of studying Scripture to the world of Bible studies. Using their FOCUS approach, each step builds on the next one, leading to a fuller understanding of the passage, all within a very reasonable time frame. We enthusiastically encourage you to explore this effective and enjoyable method of Bible study!"

—**DR. O. S. HAWKINS**, president of Guidestone Financial Resources, and **SUSIE HAWKINS**, author and longtime member of Southern Baptist Convention Pastors' Wives

"The Bible is the living and active Word of God—but it can be intimidating. Thankfully Katie and Chris take the reader by the hand, discipling them in Bible study methods. With the FOCUSed15 approach, in just 15 minutes a day, anyone can taste and see that the Lord is good."

—**HEATHER MACFADYEN**, host of the God-Centered Mom podcast

"Chris and Katie Orr have the gift of writing relatable, rich Bible studies that not only reveal the Scriptures in new ways but also teach me how to keep studying them on my own. The FOCUSed15 studies are simple enough for me to complete even when my schedule is crazy, and yet they are deep enough to allow me to linger in the Word as well."

—**KAT LEE**, author of *Hello Mornings* and founder of HelloMornings.org

"Katie Orr's Bible studies are always on my short list of recommendations. Our church has gone through several of her studies, and I was very happy to see that she (and her husband Chris) had produced another study, this one on Philippians. Her studies do something most others don't: they force you into the Bible, and that makes them absolutely priceless. Pick up a copy for yourself—or better yet, grab a handful and dive into the Word with your friends. You'll be glad you did."

—**ELYSE FITZPATRICK**, author and conference speaker

OTHER BOOKS IN THE

FOCUSed15 Bible study series

EVERYDAY *faith*
Drawing Near to His Presence

EVERYDAY *hope*
Holding Fast to His Promise

EVERYDAY *love*
Bearing Witness to His Purpose

EVERYDAY *peace*
Standing Firm in His Provision

EVERYDAY *obedience*
Walking Purposefully in His Grace

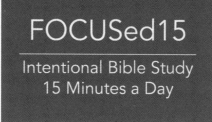

FOCUSed15
Intentional Bible Study
15 Minutes a Day

PHILIPPIANS

Engage God's Purposes.

Encounter His Peace.

Experience Renewed Joy.

CHRIS and KATIE ORR

NEW HOPE®
PUBLISHERS

BIRMINGHAM, ALABAMA

New Hope® Publishers
5184 Caldwell Mill Rd.
St. 204-221
Hoover, AL 35244
NewHopePublishers.com
New Hope® Publishers is a division of Iron Stream Media®.

Library of Congress Cataloging-in-Publication Data

Names: Orr, Katie, 1978- author.
Title: Philippians : engage God's purposes. encounter his peace. experience
 renewed joy. / Katie Orr and Dr. Chris Orr.
Description: First [edition]. | Birmingham : New Hope Publishers, 2017.
Identifiers: LCCN 2017033378 | ISBN 9781625915344 (permabind)
Subjects: LCSH: Bible. Philippians--Textbooks.
Classification: LCC BS2705.55 .O77 2017 | DDC 227/.60071--dc23
LC record available at https://lccn.loc.gov/2017033378

ISBN-13: 978-1-62591-534-4

N184107 • 1217 • 3M1

CONTENTS

APPENDIX

INTRODUCTION

THIS IS THE first book we've written as a couple. Together, we've raised babies, laid kitchen tile, and led in various ministries. We've also each separately published quite a few words on our own. As you can imagine, writing this study has been an entirely new partnership for us.

I (Katie) used to hate group projects in school. As a bit of a perfectionist, I didn't enjoy having others on my team. They slowed me down. I would typically end up doing most of the work, but I wouldn't get to do it my way, since I had to involve others. It took a long while for me to realize that what I could produce on my own would never be as good as what several competent heads put together could create. I now clearly see that collaboration typically brings about the best product. The more time spent and qualified minds that can interject their strengths into a project, the better the end production.

From figuring out who would write what to the logistics of to how to physically merge our assigned words to allowing our own voices to come through on each page, writing together has been a challenge from day one. It's caused us to better communicate and coordinate as we juggled schedules and shared kid-duty. This project has given us a goal to work toward that has stretched and challenged our relationship in ways not yet seen in our 14 years of marriage.

Yet the partnership doesn't end there. These words have passed the hands of many editors who corrected our grammar errors, pointed out the teachings that weren't quite as clear as we thought, and provided ideas to make the journey you are about to take even better. The partnership continues and the end product you hold in your hands is better for it.

Many think of the Book of Philippians as the book of joy. The words *joy* or *rejoice* are mentioned many times in the book as Paul encourages the church at Philippi to walk out their newfound faith—with joy. Even after a quick read of Philippians, the need for joy can't be missed. Yet we see another dominant theme in Philippians, though it may not readily be caught at first-glance—partnership. Not only of the partnerships within the church and between church and missionary—both of which we will see displayed in this letter to the church at Philippi—but also of the more important partnership between God and the Christian to bring about the sanctification of our souls.

This partnership is often either ignored or misunderstood. Many believe that sanctification—the process of becoming more and more like Christ—is completely up to us. We must work for it and thus prove our worthiness in the kingdom of God. On the other side of the spectrum are those who have come to faith in Christ and believe change will come automatically, without effort. Anything that doesn't change must not need changing.

These contending traps of strict legalism and moral licentiousness are both equally damaging to the name of Christ and the message of the gospel. We all have lingering desires and habits from our days before Christ that must be dealt with. However, a long, hard look at the hold those very same patterns have on us can be enough to make many throw in the towel. It's tempting to either do nothing or try doing it all. Both of these routes resemble the dysfunctional group projects I was involved in.

This Christian life is hard. Paul knew this. He experienced hardship like most of us will never have to go through. Yet, he continually chose Christ. Again and again and again, he walked forward in obedience and worship of the Savior he had come to treasure so dearly. Paul saw clearly what many of us are still trying to figure out: God is continually at work within us to make us more like His Son. Additionally, we too must work toward that goal. On our own efforts, we can only attempt to clean ourselves up in superficial ways. Propelled by the partnership with what God has already begun to do, we can ride the waves of change within our souls, positioning ourselves to hold fast to His ways as the tide of His will brings about transformation.

So, yes, Philippians is about joy. It is also about sacrifice and suffering, hard work and matters of the heart, individual pursuits and churchwide implications. The thread weaved through it all is the collaboration of a mighty God with His beloved people. A work that—though we have an important part to play—is initiated, carried, and completed by our faithful God.

We're excited you've decided to take this journey through Philippians with us! Let's get started.

THE NEED FOR FOCUS

IF THIS IS your first FOCUSed15 study, you'll want to carefully read through the following introduction and study method instructions. After that, we'll see you on Day 1!

It's hard to focus.

In a world filled with continual demands for my attention, I (Katie) struggle to keep a train of thought. Tasks I need to do. Appointments I need to remember. Projects I need to complete.

Yeah, it's hard to focus.

Without a good focus for my days, I wander. I lack the ability to choose well and to avoid the tyranny of the urgent. Without focus, days become a blur—tossed back and forth between the pressing and the enticing.

Why Focus Matters

I felt pretty lost during my first attempts at spending time with God in the Bible. After a few weeks of wandering around the Psalms and flipping through the New Testament, I realized I had no clue what I was doing.

It felt like a pretty big waste of time.

I knew the Bible was full of life-changing truths and life-giving promises, but I needed to learn how to focus on the details to see all that Scripture held for me.

In the medical world, we depend on the microscope. Even with all the fancy machines that can give test results in seconds, the microscope has yet to become obsolete. Some things can only be discovered through the lens of the scope.

What looks like nothing to the naked eye is actually teeming with life-threatening bacteria. Even under the microscope they may not be seen at first glance. But with the smallest adjustment of the focus, the blurry cloud of the field in view is brought into focus and the finest details are revealed.

And those details matter.

You need a microscope to make a diagnosis, but the microscope itself doesn't make the discoveries. It takes a trained eye to distinguish between cells. The average person may be able to figure out how to use the microscope to find a cell and get it in focus, but without training, the beginner will not know the clinical significance of what is seen.

Similarly, when we approach God's Word, we must learn to focus on what we see and develop a trained eye to know its significance.

Ready for More

I grew up in a shallow Christian culture. Don't do drugs. Don't have sex. Don't tell lies. Read your Bible. Be a light—sold-out for Jesus. This was the sum of being a good Christian—or so I thought.

Now, I'm your typical firstborn list-checker, so the do's and don'ts worked for me . . . for a while. But as I got older and the temptations of the don'ts became more enticing, I began to wonder if this Christianity thing was worth it.

Is this really what people spend their lives chasing? Seems tiring—and ultimately worthless.

Yet, God was drawing my heart—I could undeniably feel it—but I knew I was missing something. I thought I'd check out this reading-the-Bible thing. Sure, I had read a devotional or two and knew all the Bible stories, but I didn't feel I knew God Himself.

A bit nervous, I drove to the local bookstore to buy my first really nice Bible. I excitedly drove back home, headed straight to my room, opened up my leather-bound beauty, and began to read.

. . . and nothing happened.

I'm not quite certain what I was expecting, but it sure wasn't confusion and frustration. I decided to give it another try the next day and still heard nothing. I had no clue what I was reading.

In all my years of storing up the do's and don'ts in my how-to-be-a-good-Christian box, I never caught a how or why.

For years I stumbled through my black leather Bible with very little learned on the other side of it all. Yet, God was faithful to lead and speak, and I fully believe that He can and does speak to us through His Word, even if we are as clueless as I was.

However, I also believe that God's Word is meant to be a great catalyst in our growth, and as we pursue how to better know God through His Word, we will experience Him in deeper ways.

You and I need a healthy, rich diet of God's Word in order to grow. And as we read, study, and learn to digest the Bible, we move toward becoming more like Christ. When we pursue the nearness of God, the don'ts become lackluster compared to the life-giving promises of His Word.

A FOCUSed 15 Minutes

Over time, I learned how to use incredible Bible study tools that took my time with God in His Word to a deeper level. Yet with each method, Bible study seemed to take more and more time. Certain seasons of life allow for a leisurely time in the Bible; my experience has proven most of my days don't.

As much as I would love to find a comfy chair in my favorite local coffee shop and study God's Word for hours, it is just not often possible. I'm lucky if I can get a decent breakfast in every morning before my day starts rolling. Distractions and demands abound, and many days I have not even tried to study my Bible because I just didn't have what it would take, time-wise, to get much out of it.

Until I learned to focus.

I've learned that even the busiest of Christians can learn to focus and train their eyes to discover the life-changing truths held in Scripture. No incredibly long "quiet times" or seminary degree required.

All it takes is a focused 15 minutes.

The method I will walk you through consists of 15 minutes, five days a week. We will focus on the same set of verses over the course of a week, and each day of that week we will look at the passage with a different lens to gather new insights along the way.

Two Ultimate Goals

Our prayer for you as we dive into the Bible is twofold. First, we want to work ourselves out of a job. We want you to walk away from this study a bit more confident in your ability to focus on the transformational truths of Scripture on your own.

Second, we hope you will encounter our God in a deep and meaningful way through these focused 15 minutes. The most important thing about us is what we believe about God, and our prayer is that you will more accurately understand the truths about who He is through your own study of Scripture. As you get to know our glorious God better and better each day, we think you'll see your actions and attitudes are forever changed—because of who He is.

What You'll Need

A pen to record your study notes and a journal for additional notes and any bonus study work you choose to do.

A Bible. If you don't have one, I recommend investing in a good study Bible. Visit my resources page at KatieOrr.me for solid study Bible suggestions.

Both a Greek interlinear Bible and Greek lexicon. There are in-print and free online versions for both. Check out my resources page for links.

A Few Important Notes

This is only one method. This approach is my attempt at distilling down how I (Katie) enjoy spending time in God's Word. There are other great methods both Chris and I use from time to time. Take what you can from this method and use what works for you; make it your own.

Fifteen minutes is just the starting point. Some of us are in a stage of life where we'll take 15 minutes whenever we can get it. Others may be able to carve out more time. I will give you suggestions for how to shorten or lengthen the study as needed. I think you will find yourself looking up at the clock and realizing you've accomplished a lot in a short amount of time.

Using online study tools will be of great help. You can certainly do this study without getting online; however, you will expedite many of the processes by utilizing the powerful—and free—online tools I suggest throughout our time together. I totally get that being online while trying to connect with God has its distracting challenges. Do what works for you. There is no "right" way to do this study. The only way to "fail" is to stop meeting with God.

Resist the urge to consult commentaries and study Bible notes right away. I am thankful for all the resources we have at our fingertips, but oftentimes devotionals, study Bibles, and the latest, greatest Bible teacher can be a crutch that keeps us from learning how to walk intimately with God on our own. While I do believe there is only one true meaning of each verse, God has a personalized word to speak to each of us through this study. Receiving big news from a loved one in a deliberate and personalized way means so much more than receiving the news third-hand, and when the Holy Spirit reveals a message to our hearts through God's Word, it will be something we hold much more closely than someone else's experience of God. If at the end of the week, you are still unsure of the meaning of the passage, you can then look through commentaries.

For a list of my favorite online and print resources, including Greek study tools, commentaries, cross-referencing tools, and study Bibles, check out my resources page at KatieOrr.me.

HOW TO FOCUS

OVER THE NEXT six weeks we will study Philippians together using the FOCUSed15 study method. Think of us as your Bible coaches. We will point you to the goal, give you what you need, and cheer you on—but you'll be the one doing the work.

In order for this study to be most helpful for group settings, we decided to make this a six-week study on some of the richest passages in Philippians. Here is where we're headed:

- **Week 1**   Philippians 1:6–11
- **Week 2**   Philippians 1:20–26
- **Week 3**   Philippians 2:1–8
- **Week 4**   Philippians 2:12–16
- **Week 5**   Philippians 3:7–11
- **Week 6**   Philippians 4:4–9

We also wanted to have an option available to study the entire book, so we've included bonus study weeks, where we give you a bit of direction for each day's study. The bonus weeks follow the main lessons, beginning on page 154.

- **Bonus Week A**   Philippians 1:1–5
- **Bonus Week B**   Philippians 1:12–19
- **Bonus Week C**   Philippians 1:27–30
- **Bonus Week D**   Philippians 2:9–11
- **Bonus Week E**   Philippians 2:17–30
- **Bonus Week F**   Philippians 3:1–6
- **Bonus Week G**   Philippians 3:12–16
- **Bonus Week H**   Philippians 3:17—4:3
- **Bonus Week I**   Philippians 4:10–14
- **Bonus Week J**   Philippians 4:15–23

The FOCUSed15 method may be different from other studies you've completed. We're focusing on quality, not quantity. The goal is not to see how quickly we can get through each verse but how deeply we can go into each verse and find everything we can about what is portrayed. This is how we can go deeper, in as little as 15 minutes a day, by looking at the same passage over the course of several days, each day using a new lens to view it. We're not trying to get everything we can out of the passage the first time we sit in front of it. Instead, we'll come back to it again and again, peeling back each layer, 15 minutes at a time.

The FOCUSed15 Bible Study Method

For me (Katie), high school history homework typically consisted of answering a set of questions at the end of the chapter. I quickly found that the best use of my time was to take each question, one at a time, and skim through the chapter with the question in mind. So, if the question was about Constantine, I would read the chapter wearing my "Constantine Glasses." All I looked for were facts about Constantine.

Little did I know then, this "glasses" method would become my favorite way to study God's Word. The FOCUSed15 method is essentially changing to a new pair of glasses with each read, using a different focus than the read before. Together, we will study one passage for five days, each day using a different part of the FOCUSed15 method.

- ▪ **Day 1**   Foundation: Enjoy Every Word
- ▪ **Day 2**   Observation: Look at the Details
- ▪ **Day 3**   Clarification: Uncover the Original Meaning
- ▪ **Day 4**   Utilization: Discover the Connections
- ▪ **Day 5**   Summation: Respond to God's Word

For each day in our study, we will guide you through a different lens of the FOCUSed15 study method, designed to be completed in as little as 15 minutes a day. There are also bonus study ideas with every day, providing ways to spend more time and dig even deeper if you can. We'll pray together each day, declaring our dependence on the Spirit of God to open the eyes of our hearts to the truths in God's Word.

Foundation: Enjoy Every Word

Many of us are conditioned to read through Scripture quickly and are often left having no idea what we just read. So, to kick off our studies, we will write out our verses. Nothing too fancy, but an incredibly efficient way to slow down and pay attention to each word on the page.

Observation: Look at the Details

With our foundation work behind us, we'll spend the next day looking for truths in God's Word. This is a powerful use of our time; we cannot rightly apply the Bible to our lives if we do not accurately see what is there. Observation is simply noting what we see by asking ourselves a set of questions. We're not yet trying to figure out what it means, we are simply beginning an assessment. I will guide you along the way as we look for specific truths like, "What does this passage say is true about God?"

Clarification: Uncover the Original Meaning

This is going to be fun. We'll take a peek at the original language of the verses. Our three passages are in the New Testament, so we'll look up the original Greek they were written in. To do this we'll follow three simple steps:

Step 1: DECIDE which word you would like to study.

In this step, we will look for any repeated words or key words to look up, choose one, and learn more about it.

Step 2: DISCOVER that word as it was originally written.

Next, using an interlinear Bible, we'll find the original Greek word for the English word we chose in Step 1.

Step 3: DEFINE that word.

Finally, we will learn about the full meaning of each Greek word using a Greek lexicon, which is very much like a dictionary. We'll walk through an example together each week. You can also bookmark How to Do a Greek Word Study in the appendix for your reference throughout the study.

Utilization: Discover the Connections

> *The infallible rule of interpretation of Scripture is the Scripture itself: and therefore, when there is a question about the true and full sense of any Scripture . . . it must be searched and known by other places that speak more clearly.*
> —THE WESTMINSTER CONFESSION OF FAITH

Ever notice the little numbers and letters inserted in your study Bible? Most have them. The numbers are footnotes, helpful bits of information about the original text. The little letters are cross-references and important tools for study.

Cross-references do just that, referencing across the Bible where the word or phrase is used in other passages. They may also refer to a historical event or prophecy significant to the verse you are studying.

Together, we will follow a few of the cross-references for each of our passages, as they will often lead us to a better understanding of the main teaching of our verses. If your Bible doesn't have cross-references, no worries! I will provide verses for you to look up and refer you to online tools for bonus studies.

Summation—Respond to God's Word

A respectable acquaintance with the opinions of the giants of the past, might have saved many an erratic thinker from wild interpretations and outrageous inferences.
—CHARLES SPURGEON

This is when we begin to answer the question, "How should this passage affect me?" To understand this we will take three actions:

1. Identify—Find the main idea of the passage.

With a robust study of our passage accomplished, we can now do the work of interpretation. Interpretation is simply figuring out what it all means. This is oftentimes difficult to do. However, if we keep in mind the context and make good observations of the text, a solid interpretation will typically result.

This is when we will finally consult our study Bibles and commentaries! Commentaries are invaluable tools when interpreting Scripture. They are available on the entire Bible, as well as volumes on just one book of the Bible. For a list of free online commentaries, as well as in-print investments, check out KatieOrr.me /Resources.

2. Modify—Evaluate my beliefs in light of the main idea.

Once we have figured out what the passage means, we can now apply the passage to our lives. Many tend to look at application as simply finding something to change in their actions. Much in the Bible will certainly lead us to lifestyle changes, but there is another category of application that we often miss: what we believe.

We must learn to see the character of God in what we study and ask ourselves how our view of Him lines up with what we see. Of course it is helpful to look for do's and don'ts to follow, but without an ever-growing knowledge of who God is, the commands become burdensome.

3. Glorify—Align my life to reflect the truth of God's Word.

When we see God for the glorious, grace-filled Savior He is, the natural response is worship; the do's and don'ts become a joy as they become a way to honor the One we love with our lives. Worship is true application.

All of This . . . in 15 Minutes?

Yes, we know this seems like a lot of ground to cover. Don't worry! We'll be here to walk you through each day. Remember, instead of trying to go as fast as we can through a passage, we are going to take it slow and intentional. We'll look at one passage for an entire week and apply one part of the method to the passage each day.

If You Have More Time . . .

We've tried to make each day's study to be around 15 minutes of work. Because we know that some days allow for more time than others, we want to give you additional assignments you can enjoy if time allows. If you complete a day and find you have some extra time, complete the "If You Have More TIme . . ." portion

The Cheat Sheet

At the end of many of the studies, we've included a "cheat sheet." While trying to complete a Bible study, we've found that many often find themselves paralyzed with wondering, *Am I doing this the right way?* The cheat sheet is there for you to use as a reference point. It is not a list of correct answers, however, and is meant instead to provide just a little bit of guidance here and there to let you know you are on the right track.

There are also several references in the appendix you may want to consult throughout our time together. If you are new to Bible study, you might consider spending a day to read through the appendices before beginning your study. We hope those pages will be of great help to you.

Points to Ponder

For each section of Philippians (bonus weeks included) I (Chris) have provided some important themes and application points for each section. These points are designed to summarize some of the concepts from the week's passage. These points are not intended to be the answer key for the week. If you don't arrive at each of these conclusions, your study was not in vain. In fact, we hope you will come to discover additional points as a result of your study.

A Note to the Overwhelmed

Bible study is not a competition or something to achieve. It is a way of communicating with our magnificent God. If you have little time or mental capacity (We've been there, parents with little ones!), ignore the bonus study ideas and enjoy what you can. Keep moving through the study each day, and know that you have taken a step of obedience to meet with God in His Word. Other seasons of life will allow for longer, deeper study. For now, embrace these precious moments in the Word and remember that Jesus is your righteousness. When God looks at you—overwhelmed and burned-out though you are—He sees the faithful obedience and perfection of Christ on your behalf, and He is pleased. Rest in that today, weary one.

WEEK 1

In Christianity God is not a static thing—not even a person—
but a dynamic, pulsating activity, a life, almost a kind of drama.
Almost, if you will not think me irreverent, a kind of dance.

—C. S. LEWIS, *MERE CHRISTIANITY*

I (KATIE) AM not much of a dancer. I had one year of tap dance lessons as a cute four-year-old and a short stint of Friday night line dancing in high school, but that's about it. Rhythm is not in my genes, and grace is not in my movements. Part of my problem with dancing is that I overthink things. I try too hard. Instead of simply listening and responding to the music, my left-brain analytical bent goes nuts and tries to turn dancing into a formula.

Additionally, I have an independent streak, which doesn't lend naturally to partner dancing (just ask Chris). I try too hard to get the steps correct and sometimes try to move us the direction I want to go. But when I relax my movements and follow his lead, dancing becomes enjoyable and easy. I don't have to think about where we're going. I simply need to stay positioned to be led.

There is much about the Christian life that can seem, at first glance, complicated and difficult, when in reality it can be simple and natural. Walking with God is much like dancing. He is leading. He knows all the right moves. He is full of grace and beauty. Our job is to follow well.

God is the worker, we are the responder, and the Holy Spirit is our power source. We must stay plugged in. We're praying the truth you uncover in this week's study will sink deep down into your heart, resulting in a more intimate walk with God.

FOUNDATION

[FOCUSING ON PHILIPPIANS 1:6–11]

And I am sure of this, that he who began a good work in you
will bring it to completion at the day of Jesus Christ.

—Philippians 1:6

IF YOU GO into our garage, you will find a messy assortment of sporting equipment, tools, Christmas decorations, kids' bicycles, and storage bins. You will also find the scattered remnants of projects in various stages of completion. I (Chris) am really good at starting projects. Scary good. I can start a project so quick it will make your head spin. The problem is I am not very good at finishing those undertakings. Either I lose interest or run out of resources to finish, leaving our garage brimming with the remnants of forgotten projects.

Sometimes it is easy to feel as though God has forgotten about us. When we first come to faith everything is so exciting. The newness of our faith is nearly impossible to contain. As life carries on, we settle into our routines, and we begin to experience spiritual peaks and valleys, common for all Christians. Oftentimes in those valleys, our faith tends to stagnate, life grows stale, and we question whether or not God even cares. Of course, we would never admit that to anyone, but these thoughts lurk in the backs of our minds.

"[God] has granted to us his precious and very great promises, so that through them you may become partakers of the divine nature" (2 Peter 1:4). We are given many promises in Scripture, and one of these precious gems will be uncovered this week: God has begun a good work in you. He will complete it.

Because, unlike mankind, God always finishes what He starts.

1. Before we dive into Philippians 1:6–11, spend a moment in prayer. Thank Him for the work He has begun in your heart. Ask Him for a greater faith and awareness in His continual work. Praise Him for His faithfulness.

Enjoy Every Word

Today we'll work through our first layer of studying Philippians 1:6–11 by copying the passage. This exercise is designed to help us slow down and begin to grasp what is going on in this passage. Reading the passage with intentionality creates an awareness that allows for better understanding. You can write out the verses word-for-word, diagram each sentence (if you enjoy that type of thing!), or draw pictures or symbols to help you begin to understand what is being said. There is no right or wrong way to do this. Although, be careful not to jump to interpretation. Simply write what you see. This is an exercise of intentionally taking in each word. We'll build on what we learn from this practice throughout the rest of the week.

2. Read Philippians 1:6–11, and copy the verses below.

6... Being confident of this very thing, that He who has begun a good work in you will complete it until the day of Jesus Christ; 7 just as it is right for me to think this of you all, because I have you in my heart, inasmuch as both in my chains and in the defense and confirmation of the gospel, you all are partakers with me of grace. 8 For God is my witness, how greatly I long for you all with the affection of Jesus Christ. 9 And this I pray, that your love may abound still more and more in knowledge and all discernment, 10 that you may approve the things that are excellent, that you may be sincere and without offense till the day of Christ, 11 being filled with the fruits of righteousness, which are by Jesus Christ, to the glory and praise of God.

3. Write out any questions you have about this passage. Your questions should be answered by the end of the week, as you continue to study. If not, you'll have an opportunity to consult commentaries later.

We can be confident not only in God's ability to do a mighty work but also in His faithfulness to complete what He's started. No matter how messy your life is, God can bring lasting change. He is a good Father, mighty Warrior, and trustworthy Advocate.

Lean on Him. His promises are sure.

{God, I am overwhelmed by Your grace for me. I do not deserve it. I never will. Just as His great love for You fueled Christ to become obedient to the point of death on a Cross, may the same love compel me toward a life of holiness. By the power of Your Spirit, I long to live a life of worshipful obedience.}

IF YOU HAVE MORE TIME . . .

Foundation

Write out Philippians 1:6–11 onto a few 3-by-5 cards in your favorite translation. Keep the verses with you and/or post them around your house, and commit them to memory.

OBSERVATION

[FOCUSING ON PHILIPPIANS 1:6–11]

I am the vine; you are the branches. Whoever abides in me and I in him, he it is that bears much fruit, for apart from me you can do nothing.

—John 15:5

THE FIRST HOUSE we ever bought was an end unit, three-bedroom townhouse in Jacksonville, Florida. On the south side of the house was an itty-bitty yard in which sat a pathetic, little citrus tree. For the first year we lived there, we were skeptical about trying out the tree's fruit because we could not figure out exactly what kind of citrus tree it was. Our neighbors tried to convince us it was a lime tree, but these "limes" were larger than most oranges. We finally attempted to taste the pale green orbs ourselves, with very disappointing results. The rind was tough, the pith was way too thick, and the insides were dry and tasteless.

Some ten years after we sold that townhouse, we were taking a drive and decided to make a detour through the old neighborhood. Someone must have finally had the nerve to put that sickly tree out of its misery because it was nowhere in sight. We are in no way farmers, but we did learn a valuable lesson from that tree: sick trees produce sick fruit.

Scripture often talks about our spiritual development in agricultural terms, and there are many biblical portraits of fruit (either good or bad) as the produce of our lives. In our passage this week we see one of these snapshots: God's work in us produces a good and increasing fruit.

1. Open your time with God through a prayer, expressing your thankfulness for His work in your life. Ask the Holy Spirit for His wisdom and revelation as we dive deeper into the truths held in these verses.

Look at the Details

2. Begin today's study with another reading of Philippians 1:6–11. You might consider using a different version of the Bible than you used yesterday, for a fresh perspective.

3. Now, back with your preferred study version, let's take a deeper look at Philippians 1:6, looking for what is true about God. Read this verse again, and fill out the following chart.

TRUTHS ABOUT GOD

4. Let's take a deeper look at the requests Paul makes in his prayer. Read verses 6–11 with an eye focused on any petitions Paul made on behalf of the church.

PETITIONS OF PAUL

God's work within His people always leads to an increase in the "fruit of righteousness." This fruit is evidence of the righteousness of Christ within the believer. It is not a righteousness we can come up with on our own (as we will see later in Philippians), but it is a righteous that comes through faith. When our salvation happened, an inward transformation also occurred, and now our days are to be filled with the fruit of that new identity. We are no longer sick and dying trees putting out nasty fruit. We are now forever planted in the thriving orchard of God's kingdom, and when we are deeply rooted in the rich soil of His good character, we will naturally harvest life-giving, good-tasting fruit, which will bring glory and praise to our Master.

{God, I long for the fruit of righteousness to be evident in me more and more each day. I confess my life often shows more of the sick fruit from my days before You than the new fruit provided to me through Christ. Search my heart and show me where I am relying on my old, sickly way of living. Lead me into a deeper and deeper dependence on the nourishment only Your Word and Your presence can give.}

IF YOU HAVE MORE TIME . . .

Observation

Observe the relationship of Paul and the church at Philippi. Read through the passage again, noting all of the emotions and descriptive phrases Paul mentions when he addresses the Philippians.

CLARIFICATION

[FOCUSING ON PHILIPPIANS 1:6–11]

The unfolding of your words gives light; it imparts understanding to the simple.

—Psalm 119:130

ANY TIME YOU buy an item with a product manual or user's guide, it often comes in several languages. Manufacturers do this as a cost savings measure so they don't have to repackage their product for every market. While you can try to set up your new television using the Japanese instructions, why would you if you had the choice to read those same instructions in English?

This is the approach many take when it comes to the original languages of the Bible. Many see a Greek or Hebrew word, and their eyes glaze over as if they have turned to the wrong section of the user's guide. Yet, studying the original language of the Bible can deeply enrich your understanding of the passage—and you don't have to be an expert in Greek or Hebrew to do this. Following a few simple instructions and having a willingness to try new things is all it takes.

1. Open today's time with prayer. Thank God for the ability to read and study His Word freely. Ask the Holy Spirit to continue to open your eyes to the truths held in these verses.

Uncover the Original Meaning

We've come to our Greek study day. If this is your first attempt at Greek study or you need a refresher, we encourage you to take a look at the section in the appendix on How to Do a Greek Word Study. You can also check out the videos Katie has created to show you how to use many of the online Greek tools. Just head to KatieOrr.me/Resources for access to the videos.

DECIDE which word you would like to study.

2. To start your Greek study, look for any potential key words in Philippians 1:6–11. As you find any repeated word or words that seem important to the passage, write them down below.

Maybe you had the word *completion* from verse 6 in your list? Let's study this word together.

DISCOVER that word as it was originally written.

3. Using your preferred tool, look up the word *completion* to find the original Greek word.

DEFINE that word.

Now that you know the original word for *completion* used in verse 6 is *epiteleo*, we can look up this Greek word to better define and uncover the original meaning, using the following chart. (Remember to consult the cheat sheet at the end of this week if you need help.)

GREEK WORD:
epiteleo

VERSE AND VERSION:
Philippians 1:6 ESV

Part of Speech: (verb, noun, etc.)	Translation Notes: (How else is it translated? How often is this word used?)
verb	Used 10 times in the ESV
Strong's Concordance Number: G2005	**Definition:** to bring to an end, accomplish, perfect, execute, complete

Notes:

The exclusive work of God "among you" is made no less plain in Phil. 1:6 than the fact that the "carrying out" of this work right up to the **parousia**, i.e., the judgment, is decisive. [Gerhard Kittel, Geoffrey W. Bromiley, and Gerhard Friedrich, *Theological Dictionary of the New Testament*]

4. Use the above steps to look up at least one more Greek word from this passage. You might consider one or two of the following:

partakers (v. 7)

approve (v. 10)

filled (v. 11)

GREEK WORD:

VERSE AND VERSION:

Part of Speech:
(verb, noun, etc.)

Translation Notes:
(How else is it translated? How often is this word used?)

Strong's Concordance Number:

Definition:

Notes:

GREEK WORD:

VERSE AND VERSION:

Part of Speech:
(verb, noun, etc.)

Translation Notes:
(How else is it translated? How often is this word used?)

Strong's Concordance Number:

Definition:

Notes:

Paul understood this dance we dance with our Savior and Lord better than most. Without God, change cannot occur. Our transformation is wholly dependent on the power, provision, and completion of God. However, God has ordained His will to be done through the hard work and fervent prayers of His people. No one can dance with a stone-cold statue. We must be willing to be moved and molded to the patterns and rhythms of the symphony of God. We cooperate with God's leading through our obedient movements: a holy lifestyle and a life wholly dependent on prayer.

{God, grant me a deeper and deeper love for Your Word each day. As I enjoy and treasure Your words, use them to complete Your work in me.}

IF YOU HAVE MORE TIME . . .

Clarification

Follow the Greek study steps for additional words in Philippians 1:6–11. Print out the blank Greek chart from Katie's website, or make your own simple chart in your journal.

UTILIZATION

[FOCUSING ON PHILIPPIANS 1:6–11]

> And this is the confidence that we have toward him, that if we ask anything according to his will he hears us. And if we know that he hears us in whatever we ask, we know that we have the requests that we have asked of him.
>
> —1 John 5:14–15

THERE ARE SOME things in life you just have to do. You don't love the tasks—you may even loathe them (cleaning toilets, trimming hedges, or filing taxes)—but they must get done. But there are other times when you get to do the very things you love to do. If a friend or family member asks you to go out for coffee, to the movies, or to catch a quick game of basketball—and what they ask you to do is one of your favorite pastimes—you will jump at the chance to go along.

God loves to answer the prayers of His people when they ask Him to do the very things He says He loves. In 1 John 5:14–15, the Apostle John says that when we pray God's will we can be confident He will answer our prayers.

In our passage this week, Paul is praying God's will for the church in Philippi. God's will for this church is to increase in love, in wisdom, and in discernment. God wants them to be pure and blameless. God's plan for the people in Philippi is to experience righteousness through Christ. God desires for these believers to give Him glory and praise. So, Paul prays with boldness for the will of God to be made known in the lives of His people.

1. Pray Philippians 1:9 for yourself. Ask God to give you an abounding love for Him.

Discover the Connections

It's time for our Utilization study, where we'll simply look up verses related to any word or phrase we want to learn more about. To do this, you can use the cross-referencing letters in your study Bible or online study tool. You can also use a Bible dictionary to look up people, places, and themes in the Bible. If your Bible doesn't have cross-references, no worries, we'll always start you out with a few suggestions for your study. When you are ready to try it out on your own, there are many free online tools and smartphone apps. Check out KatieOrr.me/Resources for a list of cross-referencing tools.

2. Read Philippians 1:6–11 again to start your study.

3. Let's look at a few prayers recorded in other books of the Bible. Look up the following references, and note what you learn from each prayer. You might consider applying one or more of the FOCUS method steps to that passage, depending on the time you have for the day. I (Katie) typically enjoy listing out truths I see, especially those that help me understand the original passage I'm studying. You can write out the passage in the space provided or even look up a Greek word or two in your interlinear Bible. Just do what interests you and what you have time for!

Paul's prayer in Colossians 1:9–11

Paul's prayer in Ephesians 1:16–19

Christ's prayer in John 17:13–15

Paul's prayer here in Philippians is not haphazard. It is a purpose-filled prayer geared toward declaring his desire for God's will to be done among this church. We too can pray with the same fervency and boldness when we ask God's will to be done in our lives. There are many aspects of our walk with God that are spelled out for us in the Bible. His desire is for us to be filled with fruit of righteousness, to be known as a people of abounding love and purity, and for our lives to glorify our Father in heaven. And much, much more. As we grow in our knowledge of the Word and the will of God spelled out in it, these truths ought to naturally shape our prayer life. There is tremendous power when we pray the will of God.

{God, I am so thankful You hear the prayers of Your people. I praise You for Your power and ability to make Your kingdom come on earth as it is in heaven.}

IF YOU HAVE MORE TIME . . .

Utilization

Study the rest of Christ's high priestly prayer in Luke 17.

Look up and study the Lord's Prayer in Matthew 6:9–13.

Look up additional cross-references for words and/or phrases in this week's passage that you would like to learn more about.

SUMMATION

[FOCUSING ON PHILIPPIANS 1:6–11]

*For from him and through him and to him are all things.
To him be the glory forever. Amen.*

—Romans 11:36

HAVE YOU BEEN around a child going through their *why* phase? Any statement of fact is immediately followed by a why. At first, this phase is adorable, but it can quickly become irritating. No answer will satisfy their burgeoning curiosity. Every answer given is followed by yet another, "Why?"

Each of our children went through this phase. The discussion would start with an innocuous question like, "Why are there clouds?" and we would answer something like, "Because clouds bring the rain to water the crops." Which would immediately be followed by another, "Why?" We would attempt to answer that question by talking about the water cycle and how most living things need water to survive. This response led to another, "Why?" This path would ultimately lead us into some deep theological conversations. "Well, Sweetie, God made us dependent on water so we would learn we need Him even more than we need water." Of course, this led to another, "Why?" Finally we would come to a point of termination where we could only answer, "Because God made everything for His glory."

You see, it doesn't matter what question you ask. If you keep asking the why behind the question it will always lead to God and His glory. God's glory is the point of all of creation, all of His actions, all of His allowances. This is why we follow Him in holiness. This is why we dance.

1. Ask God to continue His work in your heart. Invite Him to search your heart and reveal any places that need changing.

Respond to God's Word

Let's take some time to slow down and digest what we've been learning by going through our Summation steps. This is when we begin to answer the question, "How should what I've learned affect me?"

IDENTIFY—Find the main idea of each passage.

2. Take a few moments to flip back to each day's study to review what you've learned this week. In the space below, write out Philippians 1:6–11 in your own words. Or simply write out what you think the main idea of Philippians 1:6–11 is.

3. Read a commentary or study Bible to see how your observations from this week line up with the scholars. (You can find links to free online commentary options as well as in-print suggestions for your library at KatieOrr.me/Resources.) As you search commentaries, ask God to make clear the meaning of any verses that are fuzzy to you. Record any additional observations below.

MODIFY—Evaluate my beliefs in light of the main idea.

Journal prayerfully through the following questions, asking the Spirit of God to enlighten and convict.

4. Do I truly believe that God is always at work in my life, even if I cannot see or feel it? Why or why not?

5. How instep am I in my daily dance with God?

Rigid and
Noncompliant

In Tune to God's Rhythm
and Following Him

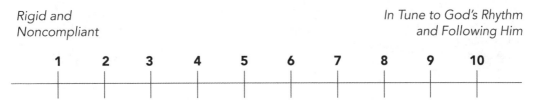

6. What are some commands of God I am not currently following?

GLORIFY—Align my life to reflect the truth of God's Word.

7. How can I pray for God's will to be done in the situations in which I am most struggling? Who is someone in my life I can ask to join me in this prayer?

8. What promises/verses can I hold on to moving forward this week to help me remember God's faithfulness and love for me?

{God, make me pliable to Your will and alert to Your movements. I long to follow You with my every thought and action. May my actions and attitudes shown today be glorifying to You.}

IF YOU HAVE MORE TIME . . .

Summation

Spend additional time in commentaries.

Add a title to this section in your outline in the appendix.

Pull out your journal and continue the conversation with God about what He is teaching you.

Share what you are learning with a trusted friend. Ask them to pray for you as you apply what you've learned.

WEEK 1: POINTS TO PONDER

[FOCUSING ON PHILIPPIANS 1:6–11]

God begins and finishes salvation.

PAUL'S CONFIDENCE ABOUT God's work in salvation is very comforting. In verse six he says God began the good work in us and He will bring it to completion. If you are a Christian, God has begun a work in you, and He will continue working until Jesus comes back or you get called home to heaven. Notice Paul doesn't say this is only true of pastors or missionaries; this is for all believers. The New Testament paints the picture that God draws people to Himself, the Holy Spirit testifies to the truth of God's Word and the work of Jesus, Jesus paid the penalty for our sin on the Cross, and God makes us alive when we were spiritually dead. Our response to all of this is faith. God is the author and perfecter of our faith, He gets all the credit and glory for salvation.

Love is often based on shared experience.

Paul defends his affection for the church at Philippi by saying he feels this way because they are "partakers with me of grace." Paul is saying they had experiences in common that bonded them together. We know this to be true personally. Katie and I were friends before we dated. It was shared experience that gave our affection room to blossom. One of the best reasons to be intimately connected to a specific local church is that you begin to share experiences with them in ways that help you grow together in love. This is not coincidental; God has designed us to work this way.

The church should exhibit supernatural love.

When you go into the supermarket you see all kinds of people. Shoppers there come in all ages, can be from various ethnic or racial groups, and can have various levels of personal wealth. What is it that bonds these people together? Nothing! When they leave the store they will likely never again be assembled with that same collection of people.

Consider a monthly quilting club for senior adult ladies. The ladies in this group probably live in similar homes, drive similar cars, and share similar political views. When the world looks at people in a grocery store or the quilting club, they have answers for why these groups have assembled. The shoppers were looking for groceries and the quilters share many interests.

But why does the world say the church assembles? Is it because we like the same music, come from the same background, live in the same neighborhood, or drive the same cars? Hopefully our communities see that outside of our commitment to the gospel there aren't many explanations for why we love the people in our churches. Supernatural love inside the church happens when we love our brothers and sisters in Christ even when we don't share many other similarities. When the church exhibits supernatural love the world takes notice.

Grow in love.

As Paul prays for the church at Philippi he specifically prays that their love would abound. Can you believe this guy? It is not enough that he wants them to demonstrate supernatural love, he also expects them to grow in love? Well actually, yes. Think about the people you love. Maybe it's a spouse, a parent, or your kids. Do you love them more now than you did a year ago? What was wrong with your love a year ago? Nothing was wrong, but as we continue to know these dear ones we grow in our capacity to love them. It is great if you love other Christians, even better if you love the people in your church. Continue to pray that God would expand your ability to love even more.

Grow in holiness.

In addition to growing in love, Paul finishes this section by encouraging this church to grow in holiness. Paul notes we are to be "pure and blameless for the day of Christ." Purity, here, refers to holiness, or our practice of right living. Paul sees holiness not as a requirement prior to salvation but as a byproduct of God working in our lives after salvation. This becomes clear as we look at his next statement that the fruit of righteousness comes through Jesus Christ. This may seem confusing, but stay with me. We don't earn our way to God by being holy. Since we can't do that, God counts Jesus' life and holiness as our own if we come to Him in faith. In one sense, because of Jesus, God looks at us as if we had never sinned. In another sense, we know that after coming to Christ we still sin. The issue is not whether our holiness comes from Christ or from our own striving. The answer is both. We are declared holy because of our connection to Christ, and we must strive to grow in holiness as our response to Christ's work on our behalf.

WEEK 1: CHEAT SHEET

Day 2: Observation

3. Now, back with your preferred study version, let's take a deeper look at Philippians 1:6, looking for what is true about God. Read this verse again, and fill out the chart below.

TRUTHS ABOUT GOD

He began a good work in me

He will bring it to completion

at the day of Jesus Christ

4. Let's take a deeper look at the requests Paul makes in his prayer. Read verses 6–11 with an eye focused on the petitions Paul made on behalf of the church.

PETITIONS OF PAUL

That your love may abound more and more with knowledge and all discernment

You may approve what is excellent

You may be pure and blameless

for the day of Christ

You may be filled with the fruit of righteousness that comes through Jesus Christ to the glory and praise of God

WEEK 2

When Christ calls a man, he bids him come and die.

—DIETRICH BONHOEFFER, THE COST OF DISCIPLESHIP

IT'S TAKEN ME (Katie) a very long while to embrace the title of writer. I have a science degree and thrived in the College of Sciences and Mathematics at Auburn University. Even in high school, I loved all things science and math. But English grammar and writing? Not so much. In fact, the worst grade I received at Auburn was from a basic freshman English class. I despised writing papers. I never, ever dreamed of being a writer.

Looking back on my writing journey, I can see a definitive moment early on where I chose to finally call myself a writer. Once I did, something inside me shifted. Moving forward, this declaration to resolutely and intentionally follow the calling to write changed the outlook of my days and shaped my decisions for how I spent my time and resources.

We all have these callings that influence the way we live out our days. Most of us have many callings on our life that shape who we are, though many of us do not clearly understand the callings bestowed on us when we decided to follow Christ.

Paul's callings were crystal clear. He had a very specific personal calling to preach what he called the mystery of the gospel—that Christ had come to save not only the Jews but all mankind. But he also knew well the corporate callings of the Christian. This week we will see three of those callings: the sojourner, servant, and satellite of God's glory. These callings profoundly shaped his every moment.

We too are called to these identities. This week we'll take a deeper look at each identity and how they affected Paul's actions. We pray these callings will shape your moments as well.

FOUNDATION

[FOCUSING ON PHILIPPIANS 1:20–26]

So, whether you eat or drink, or whatever you do, do all to the glory of God.

—1 Corinthians 10:31

ONE OF THE greatest technological advances in the twentieth century was the invention of the satellite. Satellites are used for many forms of communication—from photography to navigation—but are most well known for providing televisions with content. For most of the last decade, our family has lived so far out in the country that cable providers won't come to us; our only option has been to mount a satellite dish on the roof of our house.

Satellite technology is truly fascinating. Information from the ground is beamed thousands of miles into the sky. This information is received by the satellite, which provides a signal boost to it and then bounces it back to a metal dish attached to our roof, and our channels appear on the TV screen.

The thing about satellites is they don't actually provide any content of their own. If you opened up a satellite you would not find reels of sitcoms, documentaries, dramas, or infomercials. Satellites don't provide data, they simply relay information from the source.

In the same way Paul views himself as a reflector of God's glory. Paul's goal is for Christ to be honored in every circumstance of his life. Paul rightly understands he has no glory of his own to show the world, but through his right choices he can reflect God's glory to others.

1. Before we dive into Philippians 1:20–26, spend a few moments in prayer. Ask God to open your eyes to the life-changing truths in this passage.

Enjoy Every Word

2. Once again, for our Foundation day, we'll work through the first layer of this week's section of Philippians 1:20–26. Write out the passage below.

3. Which words or phrases in Philippians 1:20–26 stand out to you?

4. Record any questions you have about this passage.

Whether we realize it or not, we are always reflecting someone's glory. Be it our earthly heroes and mentors, our own projection of the person we wish we were, or (as we are designed to do) the radiance of Christ, we are continually beaming someone's show. Paul stood resolute in his calling to be a satellite of God's glory. Every action and attitude was laced with the desire to bring fame to God's name.

{God, reveal to me where I am seeking my own glory, more focused on matching the patterns of this world over the example of Christ. Strip away anything that clouds or distorts Your glory in my life. Make me a clear and beautiful signal of Your love.}

IF YOU HAVE MORE TIME . . .

Foundation

Write out Philippians 1:20–26 onto a few 3-by-5 cards in your favorite translation. Keep the verses with you and/or post them around your house, and commit them to memory.

OBSERVATION

[FOCUSING ON PHILIPPIANS 1:20–26]

> Do not lay up for yourselves treasures on earth, where moth
> and rust destroy and where thieves break in and steal, but lay
> up for yourselves treasures in heaven.
>
> —Matthew 6:19–21

LAST YEAR WE bought a used pop-up camper. Though tiny, it has everything our family of five needs to set up camp for a few days and spend time together in nature. In our short time as campers, we've learned not all campgrounds are equal. Some are full of well-kept, shaded, level campsites with nice, clean bathrooms. Other sites are filled with bumpy, overgrown lots situated a long distance from nasty restrooms.

If we found ourselves camping in one of the less desirable sites there are some things we could do to improve the situation. We could rent a bulldozer to level the site and buy some established trees to plant around the site. We could even hire a contractor to build another shower facility close by. Of course, to do these things would be insane. These modifications would take months to pull off and cost several hundred thousand dollars. No one would do this to modify a campsite for a two-day stay because—though it may be home for a short time—it is ultimately not our true home.

Paul understood that this earth was not his home. This life is a layover, and he was waiting for the final destination. His citizenship did not belong to this world but to a greater, heavenly kingdom. He was merely a sojourner—a camper pitched in a tent at a temporary campsite. His real home is with Jesus.

1. Open your study time with a request for more of an eternal perspective. Ask God to show you where you are wasting time and resources to make this earthly campsite a permanent home instead of spending your life in eternal purposes.

Look at the Details

2. Read Philippians 1:20–26, looking for any hints of Paul's calling and identity as a sojourner, servant, and satellite. Fill in the following chart with what you find.

SOJOURNER

SERVANT

SATELLITE

In this hypothetical situation, Paul pondered what he would do if God gave him the option to go to heaven immediately or stay on earth and continue in ministry. He came to the conclusion that both were good options. Both would bring glory to God. Though his greatest desire was to be with Christ, he also had a great longing to serve the church and bring greater glory to God through more time on earth. If he lived he did so for Christ. If he died, it was for his gain because then he would be with Christ.

{God, I confess my desire to "depart and be with Christ" is not often my greatest longing. My heart is distracted by the cravings of this world— my comfort, my pleasure, and my plans. Lord, overhaul my heart. Make it beat for You alone. Grant me a great focus to fulfill the calling as sojourner, servant, and satellite. For Your glory alone.}

IF YOU HAVE MORE TIME . . .

Observation

Create a chart to compare and contrast the two options Paul hypothetically considered.

OPTION 1: TO LIVE	OPTION 2: TO DIE

CLARIFICATION

[FOCUSING ON PHILIPPIANS 1:20–26]

This is how one should regard us, as servants of Christ and stewards of the mysteries of God.

—1 Corinthians 4:1

HAVE YOU EVER walked into a messy room and found the mess-maker still there? You probably said something like, "Clean this up, I'm not your maid/butler!" In our society, not many aspire to the role of professional butler. However, this has not always been the case.

We both enjoyed watching the hit PBS series *Downton Abbey*. Any watcher undoubtedly learned much about the dynamics of early 1900s British nobility and their staff. The house staff was enormous, and each servant took great pride in their work. Perhaps none more so than the butler.

Downton Abbey's butler, Mr. Carson, took much care and attention to every detail of his job because it was a part of his core identity. He was proud to be the butler of Downton Abbey and a servant of the Crawley family.

Paul also prided himself as a servant of Christ. His mission in service of Jesus was to help the church at Philippi to grow in their faith. Paul was committed to do whatever it took to be successful in his calling as servant.

1. Begin with a prayer of dedication to live your life today as a servant of God.

Uncover the Original Meaning

We're back again at the original Greek. We know this day can seem daunting and difficult, especially if this is a new skill for you. Just as learning to ride a bike or figuring out the latest technology can be frustrating at times, the rewards of leaning in and continuing on are worth it! If the thought of studying the Greek is still overwhelming for you, consider selecting a few words to look up in the dictionary, then rewrite the verse with the definition in place of the word you looked up. Do what works for you, but do try something!

DECIDE which word you would like to study.

2. To start your Greek study, look for any potential key words in Philippians 1:20–26. As you find any repeated word or words that seem important to the passage, write them down below.

DISCOVER that word as it was originally written.

3. Together, let's discover the original word for *expectation* in verse 20. When you find the Greek word, write it below.

DEFINE that word.

4. Fill out the following chart for the Greek word you found for *expectation*.

GREEK WORD:

VERSE AND VERSION:

Part of Speech:
(verb, noun, etc.)

Translation Notes:
(How else is it translated? How often is this word used?)

Strong's Concordance Number:

Definition:

Notes:

5. Follow the previous Greek study steps to look up at least one more word in this week's passage. Here are a few you might start with:

courage (v. 20)

desire (v. 23)

necessary (v. 24)

GREEK WORD:

VERSE AND VERSION:

Part of Speech:
(verb, noun, etc.)

Translation Notes:
(How else is it translated? How often is this word used?)

Strong's Concordance Number:

Definition:

Notes:

GREEK WORD:

VERSE AND VERSION:

Part of Speech: *(verb, noun, etc.)*	Translation Notes: *(How else is it translated? How often is this word used?)*
Strong's Concordance Number:	Definition:
Notes:	

Our hearts naturally want to be served rather than to serve. Yet "even the Son of Man came not to be served but to serve, and to give his life as a ransom for many" (Mark 10:45). Jesus held the calling and identity as a servant. If we say we follow Him, we must also follow His example of sacrifice for the sake of the salvation and growth of others.

{Lord, grant me a heart of servitude. Change my plans and goals to be those of kingdom worth. Help me to spend my days seeking not to be served but to serve others. I cannot do this alone. I need You.}

IF YOU HAVE MORE TIME . . .

Clarification

Follow the Greek study steps for additional words in Philippians 1:20–26.

UTILIZATION

[FOCUSING ON PHILIPPIANS 1:20–26]

> For the word of God is living and active, sharper than any two-edged sword, piercing to the division of soul and of spirit, of joints and of marrow, and discerning the thoughts and intentions of the heart.
>
> —Hebrews 4:12

IN ALL GOOD stories, whether read in a book or watched in a movie, you will find most share the same plot elements. Every tale has a main character—the protagonist—who encounters conflict, learns something about himself, herself, or the world through that problem, overcomes it, and then learns to live in light of the mountain they've overcome. This victory and triumph compels us and brings us back for more.

Similarly, you can also identify themes in Scripture. The Bible is not simply a collection of spiritual stories. It is one beautiful story told again and again and again through the lens of different genres and characters.

In this great masterpiece story of God, many themes emerge and repeat themselves. One of the keys to understanding the Bible is understanding the major themes of Scripture. Once you begin to see these threads running throughout the Bible they become easier to recognize, and your understanding becomes clearer. This week, we'll discuss three such themes that echo through the pages of Scripture: God's glory, our new identity as aliens, and our lives are worship.

1. Ask the Spirit of God to continue opening your eyes to these themes. Thank Him for the trustworthiness of His Word and message of love to us.

Discover the Connections

2. Read Philippians 1:20–26 once more to start your study.

3. Look up the following verses for a better understanding of Paul's heart in these words.

will be honored in my body

      1 Corinthians 6:19–20

to live is Christ

      Galatians 2:20

to die is gain

      John 12:23–25

You cannot read the Bible without seeing the proclamation of God's glory, our new identity as sojourners, and the new purpose of our lives to worship God—all truths we've seen this week—as major plot lines of the story of God. From Genesis to Revelation, these truths reverberate through each page.

{God, make these pursuits—to glorify You, seek You, and serve You—my highest aim, my deepest desire, and my greatest treasure. I love for my life to be used to publish Your story to the lost world around me who desperately need to hear it.}

IF YOU HAVE MORE TIME . . .

Utilization

Look up additional cross-references for words and/or phrases in this week's passage that you would like to learn more about.

through your prayers (v. 19)

2 Corinthians 1:11

the help of the Spirit (v. 19)

John 14:16, 26

not be at all ashamed (v. 20)

Joel 2:27

Romans 5:3–5

Look up additional cross-references for words and/or phrases in this week's passage that you would like to learn more about.

SUMMATION

[FOCUSING ON PHILIPPIANS 1:20–26]

Your testimonies are my delight; they are my counselors.
—Psalm 119:24

IN CASE OF a house fire there are only a few things you could do in those moments that could be helpful. Now, you could search Netflix for an hour-long documentary on fire to better understand how fire works or read the manuals for your fire extinguisher and smoke detectors, but these actions are not going to be very helpful in those moments. Those activities may increase your knowledge but will not help you get out of harm's way. In all likelihood, you already know what you need to do in a fire. Get out. Stop, drop, and roll if you need to first. Then get yourself and your loved ones out of the burning building.

In the same way, it is great to study the Word, gather knowledge, and have the aha moments, but at some point you need to put into action the things you have learned. This is what we call application. We grow in our faith by learning and living out the Word.

Respond to God's Word

1. Ask God to move your heart to application. Commit yourself anew to following the Spirit's leading through deliberate, obedient actions.

IDENTIFY—Find the main idea of each passage.

2. Take a few moments to flip back to each day's study to review what you've learned this week. In the following space, write out Philippians 1:20–26 in your own words. Or write out what you think the main idea of Philippians 1:20–26 is.

3. Read a commentary or study Bible to see how your observations from this week line up with the scholars.

MODIFY—Evaluate my beliefs in light of the main idea.

Journal prayerfully through the following questions, asking the Spirit of God to enlighten and convict.

4. What am I a satellite of these days?

My Own Glory   *God's Glory*

5. What do I tend to spend my time and resources on? Am I attempting to make this bumpy campsite more comfortable, or am I working toward a future in heaven?

Treasures on Earth   *Treasures in Heaven*

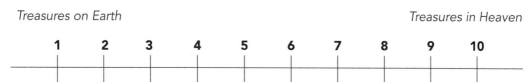

6. Do I spend my days seeking to be served or to serve?

Long to Be Served   *Seek to Serve Others*

GLORIFY—Align my life to reflect the truth of God's Word.

7. What is one adjustment I can make to better reflect the glory of God instead of my own?

8. Take a critical look at your calendar and spending habits. Ask God to show you what needs to change. Write it down below.

9. Think through the next few days and whom you will encounter. Brainstorm a few ways you can serve them. Choose at least one to implement as soon as you are able.

{God, all I have is Yours: my time, my money, my talents, my breath. Have Your way with me, Lord. Use me for Your service. Be glorified in my every moment.}

IF YOU HAVE MORE TIME . . .

Summation

Spend additional time in commentaries.

Add a title to this section in your outline in the appendix.

Pull out your journal and continue the conversation with God about what He is teaching you.

Share what you are learning with a trusted friend. Ask him or her to pray for you as you apply what you've learned.

WEEK 2: POINTS TO PONDER

[FOCUSING ON PHILIPPIANS 1:6–11]

We can be confident in the plans of God.

EVEN IN PRISON Paul was sure he would be released, one way or another. He never wavered from his belief that God would save him. Paul didn't have the ability to see the future any more than we do. How could he be so sure? We experience confidence through ordinary means. Paul points to the cause of his hope: the prayers of the church and the help of the Spirit. These are the usual ways God allows us to experience hope. Every now and then God will use special means to provide special assurance. For Paul, he experienced an extraordinary encounter with God on the road to Damascus. Other than this one encounter, Paul experienced God the way most of us usually do.

Find your purpose in Christ.

Paul views himself as primarily on earth to glorify Christ. In verse 20 he proclaims that Christ will be honored in his body one way or another. We only have one life to live, and one body to give. These were not given to us to use for our purposes alone but to use up for the glory of God. It is only when we pursue God's purposes for our lives that we actually find real meaning and purpose in life. Any other pursuit will be rendered meaningless in light of eternity. In 10,000 years no one will care about your net worth, the size of your house, or the number of friends you had. If, however, we live for Christ, we have given our lives in pursuit of an eternal treasure that will never fade.

Find your identity in Christ.

Similar to finding our purpose in Christ is finding our identity in Christ. These two concepts overlap somewhat but not completely. Finding our identity in Christ is more elusive than finding our purpose in Christ. Many people will fight for a cause for a season, only to move onto a different cause later. Those who find their identity in Christ will never move from pursuing the purposes of God, ever. Additionally, those who find their identity in Christ lose all concern for what other people think about them. When you are a beloved son of the King, who cares what anyone else thinks about you?

For Paul, to live was synonymous with Christ. He could not conceive of life apart from Christ. Jesus was his identity. This was not always the case for Paul. When we first meet Paul in the Book of Acts, he is witnessing the stoning of Stephen. The second time we see him, he is on his way to persecute Christians in Damascus. After his encounter with Christ, Paul doesn't modify his behavior or change some of his beliefs; his whole identity is changed. This radical transformation is normative for all Christians. We were all dead in sin until God made us alive in Christ. How silly is it for us who have experienced this transformation to find our identity anywhere else but the person of Christ.

Find your reward in Christ.

The second half of Paul's grand statement in verse 21 is even more audacious than the first half. He begins by saying that for him to live is Christ, but he goes on to say that death would be his gain.

Most people around the world spend an inordinate amount of time avoiding death or the thought of death. It is the fear of death that alters everything—from how our cars are made to which foods we eat. Paul has a different view of death: he welcomes it. This was not just a guy being morbid. Paul's views on death were shaped by his belief that when he died he would be with Christ. There are many songs in our hymnbooks about mansions, pearly gates, and streets of gold. What many of these songs miss is that the best part about heaven is not the accommodations but our proximity to Christ. In Paul's mind, eternity was not the reward Christ gives the faithful; rather, Christ is the reward the faithful receive in eternity. If we share this view with Paul we can have a healthy outlook on today and a proper perspective on the future.

Desire to be at home with Jesus, but wait for His timing.

In verses 22–26 Paul is wrestling with the idea of death. On one hand, if he lives he can introduce more people to Jesus and disciple more people to be like Jesus. On the other hand, if Paul dies he will be with Jesus forever. Again, we should point out that Paul was not eager to end his own life. In the end Paul knows it is not for him to decide when his life is over. Paul understands that God has left him there for a purpose, and in God's wisdom this was best for everybody. It is right that we should respond to the pain and heartache of this world by longing to be with Jesus. It would be wrong for us to move from that longing to run out ahead of God's timing and seek to end our lives on our terms. Paul strikes a healthy balance in this passage between wanting to be at home with Christ yet trusting in God's timing.

WEEK 2: CHEAT SHEET

Day 2: Observation

2. Read Philippians 1:20–26, looking for any hints of Paul's calling and identity as a sojourner, servant, and satellite. Fill in the following chart with what you find.

SOJOURNER

To die is gain (v. 21)
Desire to depart and be with Christ, which is far better (v. 23)

SERVANT

To live is Christ (v. 21)
If I live, that will be fruitful labor (v. 22)
To remain is more necessary for the church (v. 24)
I will remain for your progress and joy in the faith (v. 25)

SATELLITE

Longs for Christ to be honored in his body in live or death (v. 20)

Wants there to be ample cause to glory in Christ Jesus because of his presence among the church (v. 26)

Day 3: Clarification

4. Fill out the following chart for the Greek word you found for *expectation*.

GREEK WORD:
apokaradokia

VERSE AND VERSION:
Philippians 1:20 ESV

Part of Speech:
(verb, noun, etc.)

noun

Translation Notes:
(How else is it translated? How often is this word used?)

Only 1 usage: longing in Romans 8:19

Strong's Concordance Number:
G603

Definition:
eager desire

Notes:

Notes: Linked with ἐλπίς in Phil. 1:20, the word expresses confident expectation; the ἐλπίς denotes well-founded hope and the ἀποκαραδοκία unreserved waiting. [Gerhard Kittel, Geoffrey W. Bromiley, and Gerhard Friedrich, *Theological Dictionary of the New Testament*]

WEEK 3

The real difficulty, the supreme mystery with which the gospel confronts us, does not lie in the Good Friday message of atonement, nor in the Easter message of resurrection, but in the Christmas message of Incarnation. The really staggering Christian claim is that Jesus of Nazareth was God made man— that the second person of the Godhead became the "second man" (1 Cor. 15:47), determining human destiny, the second representative head of the race, and that He took humanity without loss of deity, so that Jesus of Nazareth was as truly and fully divine as He was human.

—J. I. PACKER, *KNOWING GOD*

MOST PEOPLE ARE unfamiliar with the name Joe Delaney, but he is perhaps the greatest hero to ever play professional football. In 1981, Delaney took the NFL by storm, winning Rookie of the Year honors and being named to the Pro Bowl in his first season. Joe Delaney's football career was off to a promising start.

After a strike-shortened second season, Delaney was enjoying a day off at an area amusement park. While there, Delaney saw three children in a pond struggling to keep their heads above water. He ran to help, and without thinking entered the waters in an attempt to rescue the children. Problem was, the football all-star had never learned to swim. One of the children scrambled to safety, but Delaney and the remaining two children drowned in six feet of water.

This star athlete willingly ran into danger for kids he'd never met. Instead of self-protection, he chose to endanger his own life for the sake of a few precious souls. The heroic act of Joe Delaney echoes the sacrifice of Christ on our behalf. Though we deserve to face punishment for our sin, Jesus voluntarily abandoned the comfort of heaven, left the presence of His Father, and gave up the rights and power due Him as part of the Holy Trinity. He chose to dive into this earth to save us. He died so we might live.

We're praying Jesus' example propels us each forward in humble actions for the eternal sake of others.

FOUNDATION

[FOCUSING ON PHILIPPIANS 2:1–8]

Finally, all of you, have unity of mind, sympathy, brotherly love, a tender heart, and a humble mind.

—1 Peter 3:8

ON DAY ONE of a new seminary class I (Chris) met several fellow pastors. We all went around the room and introduced ourselves, our families, and talked a little about the churches we served. After one man told us about his wife and children, he mentioned the name of his church—Unity Baptist Church. Immediately, I shot back at him with a question, "So when did that church go through a split?" He looked at me with some combination of shock and amazement. He responded, "How did you know we went through a church split?"

Unfortunately, through experience, I have come to suspect a church has experienced a split in the past if it has *unity* or *harmony* in its name. It may seem ironic that a church with these adjectives on their sign would be the product of a church split, but the break-up is the very thing that gave them their title. Each faction tends to see the other group as the troublemakers. From their perspective, once they've broken off from the other group, their newfound group is finally unified.

This phenomenon is all too common in church circles. Our enemy, Satan, loves to produce division in the church, and we must be constantly vigilant of his attacks. Paul knew this as well and addressed our critical need to fight for unity.

1. Before we dive into Philippians 2:1–8, spend a moment in prayer. Ask God to open your eyes to the life-changing truths in this passage.

Enjoy Every Word

ıt Philippians 2:1–8 below.

3. Which words or phrases in Philippians 2:1–8 stand out to you?

4. Record any questions you have about this passage.

The call to be unified as believers is all over Scripture. Though we may not all agree on the peripheral issues of how we worship, baptize, or the styles in which we carry out the work of the gospel, we can stand firm together in the fact that God is love, man is sinful, all are in need of Christ, and each soul must chose whom he or she will serve. These are the core teachings of the gospel, and they unite every Christian. Let us not be guilty of splitting hairs and causing dissension over our preferences.

{*God, help me to see my brothers and sisters in Christ with whom I disagree through Your eyes of love and understanding. Forgive me for where I have kept a tight fist on my preferences instead of a firm grip on the gospel. Show me how to move forward in grace and understanding for those I do not agree with.*}

IF YOU HAVE MORE TIME . . .

Foundation

Write out Philippians 2:1–8 onto a few 3-by-5 cards in your favorite translation. Keep the verses with you and/or post them around your house, and commit them to memory.

OBSERVATION

[FOCUSING ON PHILIPPIANS 2:1–8]

Do nothing from selfish ambition or conceit, but in humility count others more significant than yourselves.

—Philippians 2:3

IF YOU GO to most playgrounds across America you will find a fairly common set of equipment—a slide of some sort, a swing set, a merry-go-round, and of course a seesaw, or teeter-totter.

Children find seesaws fun for all of ten seconds. After they've had their fill of excitement on the seesaw they usually abandon it for another go on the slide. Since most kids do not know how to disembark gracefully from a seesaw, they just wait until they reach the bottom and simply hop off. The counterpart rider is at the apex of the seesaw when this happens. With no counterbalance in place, the high-flying sole passenger is now subject to the rules of gravity and comes crashing to the ground.

In a sense, the way a seesaw works is how Paul sees relationships in the church. On one hand, we are to refrain from elevating ourselves, and on the other hand, we must put others first. These are not separate actions. Just like the seesaw, you can't move down without lifting the other up, and vice versa. Only in making ourselves lower we can elevate others and put them first.

1. Ask the Holy Spirit to open your heart to His gentle correction. Declare your willingness to move forward in the humble example of Christ.

Look at the Details

2. This week's passage is filled with commands. As you head back to Philippians 2:1–8, look for the exhortations of Paul, and write them out below.

3. Read Philippians 2:1–8 one more time, this time focusing on Jesus. Fill in the chart below.

TRUTHS ABOUT JESUS	ACTIONS OF JESUS

The many commands we encounter in verses 3 and 4 are actually all part of the same command. They are each one side of the same coin, like the workings of a seesaw. In order to count others more significant than myself, I must humble myself. When I choose to not give in to selfish ambitions and conceit, I will naturally focus on the interests of others.

{Lord, sometimes I'm afraid to pray at all, much less with humility. I'm scared of where that might lead. Which just goes to show that I have elevated myself once again. I know there are opportunities every day for me to choose the needs of others over my own desires. Holy Spirit, open my eyes to see these interactions through an eternal perspective with the example of Christ as my standard. By your grace, I will chose better today.}

IF YOU HAVE MORE TIME . . .

Observation

To begin our passage, Paul lists several things the Philippian church was doing well. After commending them for what they were already doing, he called them to a deeper experience of Christ. Note what the Philippians were already doing well, according to Philippians 2:1.

CLARIFICATION

[FOCUSING ON PHILIPPIANS 2:1–8]

For you know the grace of our Lord Jesus Christ, that though he was rich, yet for your sake he became poor, so that you by his poverty might become rich.

—2 Corinthians 8:9

HOW WOULD YOU describe surrealist art? If you are a student of art you may have some helpful categories to use in describing this style of art, but for the art layman, descriptions are difficult. While it is hard to describe what makes art surreal, this type of work can be shown and observed.

Salvador Dalí is perhaps the best known surrealist artist. Even many who have no clue what surrealism is have heard of Dalí. His painting, *The Persistence of Memory* (also known as that one with the melting clocks) is a fantastic example of surrealism.

Sometimes it is easier to show an example than it is to describe something with words. Paul demonstrates this concept in our passage this week. Rather than explain, at length, what humility looks like, he simply points to our greatest example, Jesus.

1. Spend some time thanking Jesus for His obedient, humiliating walk to the Cross, which would lead to His death and Resurrection, opening up a way for you to experience eternity with God.

Uncover the Original Meaning

DECIDE which word you would like to study.

2. To start your Greek study, look for any potential key words in Philippians 2:1–8. As you find any repeated word or words that seem important to the passage, write them down below.

DISCOVER that word as it was originally written.

3. Using your preferred tool, discover the original word for *participation* in verse 1, and write it below.

DEFINE that word.

4. Fill out the Greek chart for the original word you found for *participation*.

GREEK WORD: VERSE AND VERSION:

Part of Speech: *(verb, noun, etc.)*	Translation Notes: *(How else is it translated? How often is this word used?)*
Strong's Concordance Number:	Definition:

Notes:

5. Follow the Greek study steps to look up more words in this week's passage. Here are a few you might start with:

selfish ambition (v. 3)

grasped (v. 6)

emptied (v. 7)

GREEK WORD: VERSE AND VERSION:

Part of Speech: *(verb, noun, etc.)*	Translation Notes: *(How else is it translated? How often is this word used?)*
Strong's Concordance Number:	Definition:
Notes:	

GREEK WORD:

VERSE AND VERSION:

Part of Speech: *(verb, noun, etc.)*	**Translation Notes:** *(How else is it translated? How often is this word used?)*
Strong's Concordance Number:	**Definition:**
Notes:	

The commands in these verses give a tall order. These are high callings. Thankfully, God has provided a beautiful portrait for us to model after. Through the life of Christ we see glimpse after glimpse of what our lives ought to look like, how we are to treat our enemies, and the foundations we are to build our character on—unity, humility, and sacrifice.

{God, I am so thankful I do not walk this life alone. You are with me; Your grace and Spirit enable me to walk forward in the ways that will honor You. I am grateful for the example of Christ and the fact that Jesus knows the struggles I face. He can sympathize with my weakness, yet chose perfect obedience.}

IF YOU HAVE MORE TIME . . .

Clarification

Follow the Greek study steps for additional words in Philippians 2:1–8.

UTILIZATION

[FOCUSING ON PHILIPPIANS 2:1–8]

Put on then, as God's chosen ones, holy and beloved, compassionate hearts, kindness, humility, meekness, and patience, bearing with one another and, if one has a complaint against another, forgiving each other; as the Lord has forgiven you, so you also must forgive.

—Colossians 3:12–13

IF YOU LOOK in my closet or dresser you will find some clothes I (Chris) wear all the time. T-shirts older than our kids, sweatshirts that predate our marriage, and clothes received as Christmas presents line the drawers. While these are all worn a lot, there are others that are rarely taken out of the drawers or off the hangers.

Some just don't fit like they used to. Others have gone out of style but have sentimental value. A few fit right and are still in style, but they are uncomfortable. Though some get more use than others, my ownership of an item of clothing is not affected by my choice to wear it or not. I own them all and can choose to put them on or off as I please.

All throughout Scripture are the commands to "put off/lay aside" and "put on/take on" different attitudes and actions. Our passage this week holds one such command. Though unity, humility, and sacrifice are difficult to conjure up on our own, there is a great truth tucked away in these verses. We already have "this mind" of humility through the provision of Christ Jesus.

1. Begin by thanking God for the provision of humility through the example and obedience of Christ. Ask Him to show you what it looks like to "have this mind," which is yours in Christ.

Discover the Connections

2. Read Philippians 2:1–8 to start your study.

3. Look up each of the following references, and take notes about what you learn.

though He was in the form of God/equality with God (v. 6)

John 1:1

Colossians 1:17–19

John 5:18

emptied himself (v. 7)

2 Corinthians 8:9

2 Corinthians 13:4

We are commanded to "have this mind among yourselves, which is yours in Christ Jesus." Notice Paul doesn't command believers to go out and acquire this mindset but simply to have it—take it on. It's as if the mind of Christ is a shirt already hanging in our closet. When we came to faith in Christ as our only hope, He gifted us His righteousness—we now possess every one of His perfect garments—which includes the humility He possessed (and much, much more). The mind of Christ is already ours, but we must decide to put it on.

{Jesus, thank You for Your provision of perfect obedience. I don't always understand it, and I certainly don't deserve it, but I am grateful for it. Holy Spirit, show me where I am relying on my own way of thinking instead of the way of Christ. Renew my mindset through Your Word. By Your grace I will put on the humility of Christ as a new way of thinking through my days.}

IF YOU HAVE MORE TIME . . .

Utilization

Look up additional cross-references for words and/or phrases in this week's passage that you would like to learn more about.

Taking the form of a servant (v. 7)

Matthew 20:28

becoming obedient (v. 8)

Matthew 26:39

John 10:18

every knee should bow (v. 10)

Isaiah 45:23

SUMMATION

[FOCUSING ON PHILIPPIANS 2:1–8]

For Christ also suffered once for sins, the righteous for the unrighteous, that he might bring us to God, being put to death in the flesh but made alive in the spirit.

—1 Peter 3:18

AMIDST A DOZEN kids running around, we watched the eventful 2017 Super Bowl with our church home group. The showdown was between the Atlanta Falcons and the dynastic New England Patriots. The Falcons had never won a Super Bowl. The Patriots, on the other hand, were in their seventh Super Bowl in 16 years, led by their stellar quarterback, Tom Brady. Though New England was the clear favorite, the Falcons jumped out to a commanding 28–3 lead. Atlanta was playing a good game, but New England's deficit was due to Tom Brady's poor performance. He was playing at his worst. During the lowest point of the game, Brady was devastated after having given up yet another touchdown.

Since no team had ever come back from a deficit of more than ten points in any Super Bowl, it seemed the game was in hand. In fact, many people who had gathered with us to watch the game left early to go back home. However, Brady led his team on a ferocious comeback and tied the game with less than a minute left on the clock. The Patriots won the championship in overtime. Early in the game, we saw Brady at his lowest. Celebrating his fifth Super Bowl win, we saw him at his highest. It is rare we ever get to see someone experience the lowest of lows as well as the highest of highs. It is even rarer when we get to see these intense moments happen over the course of one football game.

Christ voluntarily experienced the lowest of lows. He chose to leave the highest of highs to come as a tiny, dependent, limited baby. He walked this sin-stained earth for three decades, each day drawing Him closer to the painful and shame-filled death He knew He had to experience. All for our good and God's glory.

Respond to God's Word

1. Spend some time in worship of our Savior. Thank Him for His rescue and grace.

IDENTIFY—Find the main idea of each passage.

2. Take a few moments to flip back to each day's study to review what you've learned this week. In the space provided, write out Philippians 2:1–8 in your own words, or write out what you think the main idea of Philippians 2:1–8 is.

3. Read a commentary or study Bible to see how your observations from this week line up with the scholars.

MODIFY—Evaluate my beliefs in light of the main idea.

Journal prayerfully through the following questions, asking the Spirit of God to enlighten and convict.

4. Is being in unity with my local church body important to me? (Am I close enough to a local church body for unity to even be an issue?) What keeps me from being of the same mind and love as those around me?

5. Where am I on the humility see-saw?

Selfishness and
Elevation of Self

Counting Others More
Significant than Myself

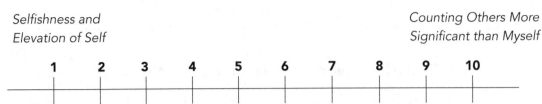

6. What issues are hardest for me to let go of my own way and put others before myself?

7. How good am I at putting on the mind of Christ?

Never Think of It

Continually Conforming
My Mind to His Ways

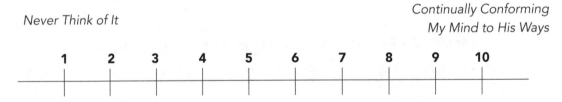

GLORIFY—Align my life to reflect the truth of God's Word.

8. Is there a particular relationship that keeps coming to mind when I think of unity? Is there someone I need to go to in humility and ask for forgiveness?

9. How can I more regularly look to the example of Christ's life and His walk to the Cross as my standard?

This life is hard. Relationships are hard. Church life is hard. But we are not left to our own devices to make things better. God has given us both the example of Jesus and the mind of Christ to utilize as we walk forward and choose a lie characterized by unity, humility, and sacrifice. And when we do, we get closer and closer to the abundant life He's promised us. Keep going. It's worth it.

{God, I need You! I cannot live a life of sacrifice on my own. But I am so thankful for all you've provided for me and promised to me. Help me keep my eyes on You more than my circumstances. Thank You for Your grace.}

IF YOU HAVE MORE TIME . . .

Summation

Spend additional time in commentaries.

Add a title to this section in your outline in the appendix.

Pull out your journal and continue the conversation with God about what He is teaching you.

Share what you are learning with a trusted friend. Ask him or her to pray for you as you apply what you've learned.

WEEK 3: POINTS TO PONDER

[FOCUSING ON PHILIPPIANS 2:1–8]

Pursue unity in the gospel.

PAUL ALSO ENCOURAGES us to stand firm in one spirit with one mind. The implication from this command is that the church might not be likely to do this. Often churches become divided over some really silly issues. Paul says to avoid division and stand firm, resisting the enemy's attempts to sever.

Find your place in ministry.

If we are not careful we will fly right by a phrase that to us sounds like a throwaway line but is really critical. This phrase, "striving side by side," is one such occasion. Paul has in mind that if he should return to Philippi and observe this church he would like to see them working together for the cause of Christ. Again, that may seem like a platitude, but having served in many churches we can tell you this is not usually the case. People often talk about the 80/20 principle in churches. This is the idea that 80 percent of the work is done by 20 percent of the people. This kind of lopsided effort is what results when people don't strive together side by side.

If you do not have a weekly job at your church, you need to get one. Many church members will have seasonal jobs, such as serving quarterly in the nursery, monthly on a committee, or singing in the Christmas choir. We are advocating that you do those things, as able, but also find a weekly opportunity to serve. If you don't have one, ask your pastor. After you pick him up off the floor from fainting, he would love to help you find such a plan to use your unique design for the cause of Christ.

Don't give into fear.

Paul is talking about the temptation to fear in the face of opponents because this church had opponents. If you stand for Christ, you will face opposition. The Bible is unequivocal on this point. On this side of eternity, you will not find an environment where everyone accepts and supports your attempt to live biblical Christianity without opposition. Jesus faced opposition. All of the disciples faced opposition. All of the prominent people in church history faced opposition. So, what makes us think we will be any different?

Suffering is not meaningless.

You may have noticed as you read through the passage that Paul attempts to calm our fears about opposition by assuring us we will suffer. In essence he is saying, "Hey there, don't be afraid, you will definitely suffer." As odd as that sounds, it can be comforting when we understand where Paul is coming from. Paul notes that suffering not only comes upon a believer but is granted to us. Who grants this suffering? God does. Since suffering has been granted to us by God we can in fact take courage. This information is comforting. Think about it. If God has no control over suffering, then we are truly helpless. But God knows about our suffering and has made promises to us in our suffering. In Romans 8:28 Paul tells us God is working all of our suffering for our good. It may not feel great in the midst of suffering but we can trust God's character enough to know that He is doing just that. These passages remind us God has a purpose for our suffering. It is not meaningless.

Suffering is not eternal.

Another component to God's granting of our suffering is knowing our suffering is not eternal. Yes, we will suffer in this life, but we will not suffer long. In eternity there is no suffering. Since Jesus paid for all our sin, there is nothing left to punish. In eternity, all that is left is to enjoy the benefits of Christ's righteousness forever. Though we will suffer now, this will all be a faint memory in glory.

Look past your own front door.

Paul concludes chapter one with encouragement about suffering. He begins chapter two with a request that the Philippians care for one another. The bridge between these two ideas is found in verse one. Paul says, "If there is any encouragement in Christ." This refers to the encouragement he was just teaching on in chapter one. He finishes that thought by talking about unity and concern for others. Salvation is an individual event, but Christianity is a team sport. We were not meant to live out our faith alone. So much of New Testament Christianity is impossible without others. Every single one of the "one another" statements in Scripture is nonsensical if we live in isolation. Since Jesus cares for us we are to care for each other.

Jesus modeled humility.

As a member of the triune Godhead, Jesus has always existed. He lived in fellowship with the Father and the Holy Spirit from all eternity past. Jesus had never experienced pain, hunger, sickness, or death. All Jesus knew was the comforts of heaven. Jesus willingly left all of those comforts to take on a human body. For the first time in history God lived as a man. This is the ultimate expression of humility.

Jesus modeled servanthood.

Jesus was born into the family of King David. Though Jesus was God and born into a royal lineage Jesus did not grow up in luxury. He worked as a carpenter in a backwater town on the banks of the Sea of Galilee for the first thirty years of His life. Jesus was a servant in every way. He served us by leaving the comforts of Heaven. Jesus served us by living among peasants. He served us by rejecting human attempts to make Him king by force. Finally, Jesus served us through His sacrificial death on the Cross. If Jesus is our Lord, how can we not serve others?

Jesus' obedience cost Him everything.

Paul says Jesus was obedient to the point of death. What does he mean by this? Jesus, as God, knew what redemption would require—He was no stranger to the plan. But on the night of His arrest we see Jesus' inner conflict boil to the surface as He prays to the Father to allow the cup of judgment to pass from Him. The picture in the Gospels is that Jesus fully understood what it would take of Him to go to the Cross and have the sin of the world placed upon Him. This thought was deeply troubling to Jesus. Fortunately, Jesus did not allow the gravity of the situation to derail His desire to do the will of the Father. Jesus submitted in obedience to the Father His entire time on earth, even though it led to His death.

Obedience to God is going to cost us; there is no way around that. Following God will cost us time, opportunity, relationships, resources, comfort, and possibly even our health and well-being.

WEEK 3: CHEAT SHEET

Day 2: Observation

2. This week's passage is filled with commands. As you head back to Philippians 2:1–8, look for the exhortations of Paul, and write them out below.

Be of the same mind (v. 2)

Have the same love (v. 2)

Be in full accord and of one mind (v. 2)

Do nothing from selfish ambition or conceit (v. 3)

Count others as more significant than yourself (v. 3)

Don't look out only for your interest, but also the interests of others (v. 4)

Have the mind of Christ among yourselves (v. 5)

3. Read Philippians 2:1–8 one more time, this time focusing on Jesus. Fill in the chart below.

TRUTHS ABOUT JESUS	ACTIONS OF JESUS
Was in the form of God (v. 6) Was equal with God (v. 6)	Didn't keep a grasp on His equality with God (v. 6) Emptied Himself (v. 7) Took the form of a servant (v. 7) Came to earth as a baby (v. 7) Humbled Himself (v. 8) Obedient to the point of death on a Cross (v. 8)

Day 3: Clarification

4. Fill out the Greek chart for the original word you found for *participation*.

GREEK WORD:
koinonia

VERSE AND VERSION:
Philippians 2:1 ESV

Part of Speech:
(verb, noun, etc.)

noun

Translation Notes:
(How else is it translated? How often is this word used?)

also translated fellowship, share/sharing, contribution, part, partnership (used 19 times total)

Strong's Concordance Number:
G2842

Definition:
communion, fellowship

Notes:

κοινωνός means "fellow," "participant." It implies fellowship or sharing with someone or in something. [Gerhard Kittel, Geoffrey W. Bromiley, and Gerhard Friedrich, Theological Dictionary of the New Testament]

WEEK 4

Let not that man think he makes any progress in holiness who walks not over the bellies of his lusts. He who doth not kill sin in his way takes no steps towards his journey's end. He who finds not opposition from it, and who sets not himself in every particular to its mortification, is at peace with it, not dying to it.
—JOHN OWEN, *OF THE MORTIFICATION OF SIN IN BELIEVERS*

THERE ARE SOME things in life that are truly complex and difficult. Take, for example, neurosurgery. We recently had a dear friend go through brain surgery to remove a tumor. Given the complexities of the human brain, you can bet he and his wife did not choose a surgeon lightly but chose someone who'd spent years learning about human brain anatomy and physiology before they were given consent to enter my friend's skull with sharp instruments. The choice wasn't all about knowledge, either. Once a doctor has completed medical school and residencies, he or she must hone their skills as a surgeon. These doctors spend hours each day in situations where a wrong move can leave a patient with lifelong damage. In surgery, mistakes are not measured in inches but millimeters. So, yes. Brain surgery is both complex and difficult.

Or consider aerospace engineering. It takes years of research and development to build an aircraft, and for good reason. A fully boarded jumbo jet carries hundreds of people and thousands of gallons of jet fuel. A design flaw in one of these airplanes can lead to disasters of epic proportions. It is fitting that the engineers who work on these planes spend years training in their field, and designers spend years testing materials. Aerospace engineering is both complex and difficult.

There are other categories of feats that are difficult but not complex. How many of us can dunk a basketball on a ten-foot regulation goal? A very small percentage of people are able to accomplish this feat. This is not to say, though, that dunking a basketball is a complex endeavor. It is simple in concept but difficult to execute.

The last group are the things that are simple but not easy. We would put living the Christian life in this category. Living the Christian life is fairly simple: love and obey God. However, faithfully living as a Christian is anything but easy. Think about the times in your life when you experienced the most spiritual growth. What were you doing during this period? Chances are you were exercising your faith vigorously. It is no coincidence that putting in the hard work necessary to live the Christian life produces the fruit we are told about in Scripture.

In the passage we will study this week, Paul encourages us to work out our own salvation. Though the gospel is simple enough a child can understand it, living as a believer takes a lot of intentional, hard work. No one grows in their faith by passively expecting change to occur.

We're praying God will give you a biblical understanding of working out your salvation through your study of His Word this week.

FOUNDATION

[FOCUSING ON PHILIPPIANS 2:12–16]

Let us hold fast the confession of our hope without wavering,
for he who promised is faithful.

—Hebrews 10:23

OUR SWEET DAUGHTER Anna is frightened of dogs. As she has grown, her fears have subsided a bit, but whenever we pass a dog at the park or visit a friend's house with a canine, you can find Anna wherever is farthest from the beloved pet.

We've tried to teach our second-born that most dogs are very friendly and simply want to say hello. However, we've also shown her how to look for a leash. If the dog is on a leash, and you stay away, it can't get to you. The presence of a leash provides a layer of protection for her.

The leash is also a protection for the dog. It serves the purpose of keeping a canine within a certain boundary, away from the dangers of the road and/or getting lost. We humans use child leashes from time to time, as well. Especially in crowded, busy situations (like a theme park), a leash can keep a curious toddler from wandering off.

The Bible is our safe and stable, good, and gracious leash. The truth of God's Word is our tether. Though it may feel confining at times, when we begin to see God's loving purpose for those restrictions, binding ourselves to the cord of biblical teaching can become a welcomed protection. In a day and age where God's ways are continually being scoffed as old-fashioned and irrelevant, we must chose to hold fast to God's good and perfect ways.

1. Pray for a deeper love for God's Word and His ways. Ask God for the grace to hold fast to the Word of life.

Enjoy Every Word

2. Work through the first layer of Philippians 2:12–16 by writing out the passage below.

3. Which words or phrases in Philippians 2:12–16 stand out to you?

4. Record any questions you have about this passage.

Just as a budget brings a security that you will reach your financial goals, the way of the Lord spelled out in His Word brings both boundaries and bounty. Protection and progress. Regulation and reward. Let's hold fast to His words that bring life.

{God, I am so thankful Your Word does not return void. You are working in me, and every minute spent with You through the Bible is continuing that great work. Give me the grace to endure in the discipline of setting aside time to study and pray and meditate on who You are. May my heart and mind be conformed to the ways of Your Word.}

IF YOU HAVE MORE TIME . . .

Foundation

Write out Philippians 2:12–16 onto a few 3-by-5 cards in your favorite translation. Keep the verses with you and/or post them around your house, and commit them to memory.

OBSERVATION

[FOCUSING ON PHILIPPIANS 2:12–16]

> You are the light of the world. . . . In the same way, let your light shine before others, so that they may see your good works and give glory to your Father who is in heaven.
>
> —Matthew 5:14–16

SOMETIMES IT IS good to blend in with the crowd. No one wants to have the only lawn in the neighborhood that hasn't been cut for weeks. No one likes to be underdressed for an occasion. No one enjoys being singled out by a boss when things aren't going well at work. In these instances, blending in with the crowd is the way to go.

There are other occasions when standing out is preferable. If you are adrift at sea and in need of rescue, you better hope you stand out from the ocean. You also want to stand out in a job interview as the best candidate. Standing out is also preferable if you operate a lighthouse on a dangerous coastline; you hope your light stands out from the darkness.

This is Paul's hope for the church at Philippi. He wants them to experience growth in the Christian life so they will shine as lights in the darkness. As Christians we are not commanded to blend in with the world but to stand out from the world. We are to shine as lights so others may come in from the danger and darkness.

1. Confess any fear or hesitation you have about standing out as a light in the darkness. Thank God for bringing the light of the gospel to your life.

Look at the Details

2. Once again, we're going to see many commands today. Read Philippians 2:12–16, and note below all the commands you find.

3. All three commands in this passage also have a why attached to them. Read Philippians 2:12–16 one more time, and look for the motivators Paul gives as fuel for our obedient working.

COMMAND	MOTIVATION

Depending on your personality, you may not like to stand out. And in today's culture, where being known as a Christian is becoming less and less of a desirable thing, the evil one would love to keep us shut up in our safe places instead of out in the limelight. Thankfully, the light we shine is not one of our own. It is not something we have to contrive on our own; it is a natural result of being with Jesus and following Him in obedience. He shines through us for the sake of those who do not know Christ.

{God, take away my fear of what others think or what privileges I might lose if I look different from those around me. Grant me a great boldness to declare Your worth to those around me who are desperate to experience Your grace.}

IF YOU HAVE MORE TIME . . .

Observation

Note what is true about God in this passage.

Note all that is true of the Christian.

CLARIFICATION

[FOCUSING ON PHILIPPIANS 2:12–16]

For this is the will of God, your sanctification.

—1 Thessalonians 4:3

OUR YOUNGEST TWO children love to work on those neon scratch-off pictures. They come in packages of 6-inch sheets of card stock completely coated with the same substance as a scratch-off lottery ticket. With a pencil or fingernail, you can create patterns and images by scratching off of the top black layer. Most of the time, instead of slowing scratching away intricate designs, our kids take a penny and scratch away furiously so they can get to the pretty picture underneath.

Like our kids with these scratch-off pictures, we must engage in the sanctifying work of scraping off and removing the remains of our former self that clouds and covers. As we rub away the sin that no longer defines and controls us, it allows the beauty of Christ within us to shine clearly to those around us.

To be clear, we cannot work for our salvation. Salvation is a gift to be received by faith, not earned by works. But this gift we've received has changed us forever. We are justified by His grace; we have been made new. But while we are still on this earth, we have much sanctifying work to do to allow this inward transformation to become evident on the outside.

1. Begin your study with a commitment to work. Ask God for the grace and strength to run this race of the Christian life with great persistence and endurance.

Uncover the Original Meaning

DECIDE which word you would like to study.

2. Look for any potential key words in Philippians 2:12–16.

DISCOVER that word as it was originally written.

3. Using your preferred tool, discover the original word for *work out* in verse 12, and write it below.

DEFINE that word.

4. Fill out the Greek chart for the original word you found for *work out*.

GREEK WORD: VERSE AND VERSION:

Part of Speech: *(verb, noun, etc.)*	Translation Notes: *(How else is it translated? How often is this word used?)*
Strong's Concordance Number:	Definition:
Notes:	

5. Follow the Greek study steps to look up at least one more word in this week's passage. Here are a few you might start with:

works (v. 13)

work (v. 13)

holding fast to (v. 16)

GREEK WORD: VERSE AND VERSION:

Part of Speech: *(verb, noun, etc.)*	Translation Notes: *(How else is it translated? How often is this word used?)*
Strong's Concordance Number:	Definition:
Notes:	

GREEK WORD: VERSE AND VERSION:

Part of Speech: *(verb, noun, etc.)*	Translation Notes: *(How else is it translated? How often is this word used?)*
Strong's Concordance Number:	Definition:

Notes:

Instead of going to the gym and putting in hours of work, how awesome would it be if we could simply outsource our gym time to someone who likes to do that sort of thing and still reap the benefits? If this were possible it would become a trillion dollar industry overnight.

Though we can dream about letting someone else work out on our behalf, the reality is that no one can work out for us. The same is true in our spiritual life. We each have a personal responsibility to work out our own sanctification, giving evidence to the internal salvation we've experienced.

{God, I confess my laziness and forgetfulness. I fail to reflect Your glory. I continually choose poorly. I am far from blameless. Yet, You chose me to be Your own possession as a light among the nations. Holy Spirit, guide and guard me as I walk in the midst of a crooked and twisted generation. Shine through me. For Your glory.}

IF YOU HAVE MORE TIME . . .

Clarification

Follow the Greek study steps for additional words in Philippians 2:12–16.

UTILIZATION

[FOCUSING ON PHILIPPIANS 2:12–16]

But now that you have been set free from sin and have become slaves of God, the fruit you get leads to sanctification and its end, eternal life.

—Romans 6:22

IMAGINE SOMEONE BRINGS you dinner in a McDonald's bag. You open the bag and inside is a beautiful New York strip steak, bright green, steamed broccoli, and a baked potato. What would you think? You would probably assume the food did not come from McDonald's. Not that McDonald's makes bad food, but a medium-rare steak is definitely not on the menu at any McDonald's we're aware of.

In the same way we can safely assume the steak did not actually come from Ronald's kitchen, we can also deduce anything gloriously surprising in our lives comes from God. Our salvation is a gift of God. Our growth in the Christian life is carried out by God. He is our strength. He gives wisdom. He is our source. So if everything comes from God, what part do we play? Why do we have to work if He is the one working?

This is the heart of Paul's discussion in our passage this week. He tells us to work out our salvation and that God is working in us. The key concept is partnership. The Christian life is a partnership between God and the believer. God works in us, and we live according to the work He does in us. As we grow in faith we love God more and enjoy sin less. God works in us to change our desires, and we work hard to live according to those godly desires and not according to our past worldly desires.

1. Spend some time in prayer, asking God to show you how you can better partner with Him to rid your moments of attitudes and actions that are not in keeping with the gift of salvation God has provided. Ask Him for the power and the desire to obey Him.

Discover the Connections

2. Read Philippians 2:12–16.

3. Look up each of the following references, and take notes of any truths that reveal a bigger picture of the threads this verse is attached to.

   For it is God who works in you, both to will and to work (v. 13)

          1 Corinthians 3:6

          1 Corinthians 15:10

          2 Peter 1:3

   without blemish (v. 15)

          Jude 24

1 Peter 1:22

Though we may not always understand the specifics, we can know this: God has worked, God is working, and this work will be completed. We live a life of faith in this work. We walk forward from a foundation of the transformation we experienced when we first came to faith in Christ. Then we spend our lifetime working out that salvation, becoming more and more like Christ every step of the way. We trust that the Lord's ways are good, and we obey so the inward realties can be seen on the outside. As we do, our lives become more and more a display of God's glory. Lights shining in the darkness.

{God, I long to be a beacon of Your glory to those around me. Forgive me for my forgetfulness and laziness. I get caught up in my comfort and settle into my old ways instead of fighting for what's best. By Your grace, I will choose better today. I will walk hand-in-hand with You, allowing Your powerful work to be carried out in my moments. For Your glory.}

IF YOU HAVE MORE TIME . . .

Utilization

Look up additional cross-references for words and/or phrases in this week's passage that you would like to learn more about.

children of God (v. 15)

Ephesians 5:1

lights in the world (v. 15)

Matthew 5:14–16

Ephesians 5:8–10

Titus 2:10

SUMMATION

[FOCUSING ON PHILIPPIANS 2:12–16]

Do your best to present yourself to God as one approved, a worker who has no need to be ashamed, rightly handling the word of truth.

—2 Timothy 2:15

NO ONE WANTS to misinterpret the Bible. It's not an intentional violation, but it happens all the time. You've done it. We've done it. And we're each susceptible to do it again.

When it comes to interpreting Scripture you might come across an interpretation for a passage, that while plausible, is incorrect. So how do we know which meaning is correct? One key element to consider when interpreting Scripture is to allow clear passages to explain less clear passages. If we do not learn to carefully interpret Scripture with other Scripture and unclear passages in light of more clear passages, we will come to conclusions that are unbiblical and unhelpful.

This week as you study verse 12 it may, at first glance, seem like Paul says we earn our salvation by working hard. Since this passage can be unclear, we must find a place where Paul more clearly lays out his understanding of salvation (Ephesians 2:1–10, for example) to get a better understanding of what he is trying to teach in this passage. It is clear from many other passages in Scripture that we cannot achieve salvation by any means. Salvation is by God's grace alone. Our only part in salvation is faith. But true saving faith always results in fruit-filled, actively abiding believers.

Respond to God's Word

1. Ask God to fully open your eyes and heart to the meaning and implications of this passage.

IDENTIFY—Find the main idea of each passage.

2. Flip back to each day's study to review what you've learned this week. In the space provided, write out Philippians 2:12–16 in your own words.

3. Read a commentary or study Bible to see how your observations from this week line up with the scholars.

MODIFY—Evaluate my beliefs in light of the main idea.

4. What is my view of Scripture?

A Book of Irrelevant Stories and Restrictive Rules   *The Active, Living Source of Abundant Life in Christ*

5. How well am I shining the glory of Christ to the dark world around me?

I Look No Different from Before I Came to Christ   *People Can Clearly See Christ in Me*

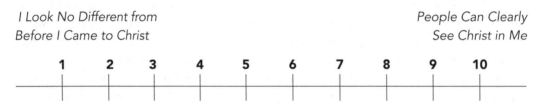

6. How actively am I working out my salvation?

Completely Inactive   *Intentional, Moment-By-Moment Obedience*

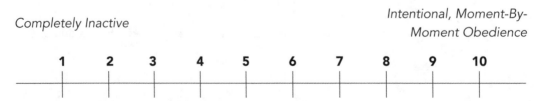

7. What is my current desire for God's Word?

Take It or Leave It   *Can't Live Without It*

1   2   3   4   5   6   7   8   9   10

GLORIFY—Align my life to reflect the truth of God's Word.

8. Are there any adjustments I need to make in the way I view the Word of God?

9. What actions do I need to take this week to better work out my salvation, shine as Christ's light, and hold fast to the Word of life?

{Holy Spirit, fill me. I am so thankful for Your continual presence within me, but I invite You right now to invade my life. Every space. Every thought. Every action. By Your power, I will walk forward in obedience to Your Word. Conform me more and more into the image of Christ.}

IF YOU HAVE MORE TIME . . .

Summation

Spend additional time in commentaries.

Add a title to this section in your outline in the appendix.

Pull out your journal and continue the conversation with God about what He is teaching you.

Share what you are learning with a trusted friend. Ask him or her to pray for you as you apply what you've learned.

WEEK 4: POINTS TO PONDER

[FOCUSING ON PHILIPPIANS 2:12–16]

Salvation is obedience to Jesus.

PAUL ENCOURAGES THE church to obey Christ, even though Paul is not there to help them. Obedience is part and parcel with New Testament Christianity. We cannot come to Christ as Savior while rejecting Him as Lord. When we come to Jesus as Savior, we trust that He alone pays our sin debt and reconciles us to the Father. When we come to Him as Lord, we allow Jesus to be the undisputed ruler in our lives. Biblically, these are two sides of the same coin. Salvation is trusting Christ as Savior and Lord. Since Jesus is Lord in the life of a believer we must do what He says. No longer are we free to do as we please, we exist to serve our master.

Salvation is a personal choice.

Notice Paul says each Christian must work out his or her own salvation. The implication is that no one can do this for you. You cannot be dependent on your pastor to drag you along toward spiritual maturity. You cannot delegate your spiritual growth to your spouse. This is an area in which that you must labor, and you alone. This does not mean others play no role in your development, but it does mean that if you aren't willing to work, you will not see the growth.

Living out our salvation takes hard work.

It is no accident that Paul uses the word *work* to describe our Christian activity. We are promised many things in Scripture, but God never promised that being a Christian would make our lives easier. Following Christ will bring forgiveness of sin, eternal life, meaning, purpose, and joy. Nowhere are we promised that being a Christian makes us immune from the hurts and struggles in this life. All of these painful experiences help us look forward to the day when we will be in glory. Until such time we must continue to do the hard work of resisting temptation, repenting of sin, maintaining spiritual disciplines, loving people, and worshipping God.

Salvation is serious business.

Paul describes the working out of our salvation as being done with fear and trembling. He is painting the picture that this is serious business. What is more important than our eternal destiny? If we take lightly these weighty matters of truth we run the risk of being separated from God forever. True believers will not just honor God with their lips but with their whole lives.

Salvation is a work of God.

This is where we must point out the difference between working out our salvation and working for our salvation. The difference here is gigantic. Working for our salvation suggests that by our effort we can earn God's love. This is a notion the Bible explicitly rejects. Paul describes the Christian life as working out our salvation. You don't work to earn biceps; you work out the biceps you already have. Similarly, we do not work for salvation; we work out the salvation we already have. So that we don't miss this point Paul says salvation is a work of God when he says, "it is God who works in you." Since God works in us to bring about salvation, we have nothing to brag about.

To be a Christian is to buy into God's plan.

How do we get to the point where we can do everything without grumbling or disputing? By buying into God's plan. When you are completely invested in doing God's will there is no room for complaint. When we take on this mindset we are able to see everything as an occasion for God's glory. What used to be seen as a major setback is now an opportunity for God to work in our lives so that He gets the credit.

To be a Christian is to stand out from the world.

Paul calls the church to shine as lights in the midst of a crooked generation. It is impossible to both shine and blend into the darkness. Lights shine in direct contrast to darkness. The call to follow Christ cannot coexist with the desire to go unnoticed. Standing out may put a target on our backs, but this should not cause us fear. What should cause us fear is getting to the end of our lives and looking just like the rest of world.

Living as a Christian requires us to believe God's Word.

In the same way that it would be impossible for light to blend into darkness it is also impossible to stand for Christ in a twisted generation without holding fast to God's Word. If we move from the Word we are like a boat with no moorings, eventually we will drift away. Christians who are not deeply rooted in Scripture will start to agree with secular culture on issues of morality. Only by refusing to budge from the Bible can we resist the winds of cultural change. This concept was true in Paul's day and still is now.

WEEK 4: CHEAT SHEET

Day 2: Observation

2. Once again, we're going to see many commands today. Read Philippians 2:12–16, and note below all the commands you find.

Work out your salvation with fear and trembling

Do all things without grumbling or disputing

Hold fast to the Word of life

3. All three commands in this passage also have a why attached to them. Read Philippians 2:12–16 one more time, and look for the motivators Paul gives as fuel for our obedient working.

COMMAND	MOTIVATION
Work out your salvation	Because God is working in you
Do all things without grumbling or disputing	So that you will be blameless and innocent lights among the wicked world
Hold fast to the Word	So that Paul's work will not be wasted.

Day 3: Clarification

4. Fill out the Greek chart for the original word you found for *work out*.

GREEK WORD:

katergazomai

VERSE AND VERSION:

Philippians 2:12 ESV

Part of Speech:
(verb, noun, etc.)

verb

Translation Notes:
(How else is it translated? How often is this word used?)

used 22 times; translated into over 10 different English words; produced is the most common translation (7 of the 22 in the ESV); Philippians 2:12 is the only place it is translated as work

Strong's Concordance Number:

G2716

Definition:

accomplish, prepare

Notes:

implying something done with thoroughness [James Swanson, Dictionary of Biblical Languages with Semantic Domains: Greek (New Testament)]

WEEK 5

When the glory of God is the treasure of our lives, we will not lay up treasures on earth, but spend them for the spread of his glory. We will not covet, but overflow with liberality. We will not crave the praise of men, but forget ourselves in praising God. We will not be mastered by sinful, sensual pleasures, but sever their root by the power of a superior promise. We will not will nurse a wounded ego or cherish a grudge or nurture a vengeful spirit, but will hand over our cause to God and bless those who hate us. Every sin flows from the failure to treasure the glory of God above all things.

—JOHN PIPER

THE MOST FAMOUS archeological discovery of the twentieth century was the tomb of Egyptian Pharaoh Tutankhamun (King Tut). While some pharaohs were buried in elaborately constructed pyramids, Tutankhamen was buried in the Valley of the Kings. The location of his burial was lost to history. Historians believe the entrance of his tomb was covered with stone chips and sand due to a flood. After the waters abated the tomb's entrance would have been indistinguishable from the surrounding desert floor.

In 1914 a British noble, Lord Carnarvon, sought to finance the discovery of Tut's burial site. (Lord Carnarvon is also famous because his home, Highclere Castle, was the set of the hit PBS show *Downton Abbey*.) Carnarvon turned to British archeologist Howard Carter to hunt for the elusive tomb. After years of searching, his party finally found a stairway buried in the desert sands of Egypt. The team painstakingly excavated a path into the final chamber.

Carter sent for his financier, Lord Carnarvon, to come witness the moment they broke through into the first and only untouched burial chamber of a pharaoh. Carter took out his trusty chisel and chipped away a small hole in the door. Holding up a candle he peered in. Lord Carnarvon famously asked, "Can you see anything?" Carter replied, "Yes, wonderful things!" The tomb of Tutankhamen was filled with more than 5,000 items that had been undisturbed for more than 2,200 years.

This week as we look at Philippians 3:7–11, we are peeking into a chamber filled with treasures beyond even the wildest imagination—and we will behold wonderful things. We pray God gives you a greater wonder and amazement concerning His Word that surpasses any affection we have for the treasures of this world.

FOUNDATION

[FOCUSING ON PHILIPPIANS 3:7–11]

Indeed, I count everything as loss because of the surpassing worth of knowing Christ Jesus my Lord.

—Philippians 3:8

IF YOU ARE applying for a job, most employers will want a résumé. While it can be difficult to put on paper the things that make you a uniquely qualified and capable person, this is the primary tool to get your foot in the door for most positions. Most résumés will include information about a candidate's education and work history. The job seeker might also include information about skills he or she possesses or projects he or she has worked on that demonstrate competence.

We understand, though, that a person is more than their education and history. For all the things on your résumé, there are many more accomplishments you wouldn't include. Things like past athletic achievements, number of kids or grandkids, missions trips you went on, or people you helped.

Paul does this in Philippians 3:4–6 when he lists his spiritual achievements. Then, in the passage we are studying this week, he compares that list with knowing Jesus. Paul concludes there is no comparison. No matter how accomplished we are in life, nothing compares to the greatness of knowing Jesus and being known by Him.

1. Begin today's study with a declaration of God's goodness. Ask Him to show you where you are treasuring the accomplishments and accolades of this world more than the presence of Christ in your life.

Enjoy Every Word

2. Write out Philippians 3:7–11 below.

3. Which words or phrases in Philippians 3:7–11 stand out to you?

4. Record any questions you have about this passage.

If you were to write out everything of value you ever accomplished, like a résumé of your life, what would you put on it? It is tempting to be defined by our earthly successes. Whether that be in the work place or home space, we all attach our self-worth and well-being to something (or sometimes someone). Only Christ and His purposes are worth our time, energy, and emotions. May we stand with Paul today and declare the surpassing worth of knowing Christ over all this world can offer.

{Jesus, You are worth it. Whatever You call me to leave behind, I will. By Your strength. For Your glory.}

IF YOU HAVE MORE TIME . . .

Foundation

Write out Philippians 3:7–11 onto a few 3-by-5 cards in your favorite translation. Keep the verses with you and/or post them around your house, and commit them to memory.

OBSERVATION

[FOCUSING ON PHILIPPIANS 3:7–11]

The kingdom of heaven is like treasure hidden in a field, which a man found and covered up. Then in his joy he goes and sells all that he has and buys that field.

—Matthew 13:44

ACCORDING TO GUINNESS World Records the most dominoes toppled occurred in the Netherlands in 2009. An astonishing 4,491,863 dominos fell one after another. It took 89 workers to place these dominoes. No doubt, those workers had nerves of steel placing piece after piece with surgical precision. With that many dominoes and workers, you can imagine the tension was high until the time came to topple the first domino.

Even if you've never attempted a world record domino event, you know it all starts with the first one. If a domino is not knocked over, the chain reaction does not take place. Only when the first one falls is the reaction set in motion. Of course, once the dominoes begin to fall there is no stopping them.

In our passage for the week, Paul describes a spiritual chain reaction. First step is making Jesus our greatest treasure. After this, our affections and actions fall behind. In Paul's mind, none of these subsequent effects can happen if we don't first see Jesus as our treasure.

1. Ask the Holy Spirit to begin gently revealing anything (or anyone) you are treasuring more than Christ.

Look at the Details

2. Let's take a deeper look at the cascade of desires recorded by Paul. Read Philippians 3:7–11, looking for the cause and effects in these verses. It may not be super clear at first glance. Pay attention to transition words like *that*, *because*, and *for*. (Don't forget about the cheat sheet at the end of this week if you get stuck.)

Our affections are a powerful force for diving into difficulties. Ultimately, we each do what we want to do.

Suffering well, losing the things we previously thought were valuable, receiving righteousness from Christ, knowing the power of Jesus' Resurrection, sharing in Christ's sufferings, and finally, resurrection from the dead all come after placing our highest value on knowing Christ.

{Holy Spirit, show me where I am treasuring something or someone more than knowing Christ. Open my eyes to the areas that need change. Help me move forward. Stir up my affections for Christ. May those affections be a powerful force for change in my life.}

IF YOU HAVE MORE TIME . . .

Observation

Note the two types of righteousness Paul names. Create a chart to gather all you can learn about each.

CLARIFICATION

[FOCUSING ON PHILIPPIANS 3:7–11]

So therefore, any one of you who does not renounce all that he has cannot be my disciple.

—Luke 14:33

DID YOU KNOW it is mathematically impossible to build muscle and lose weight at the same time? In order to build muscle you have to strain your muscles and eat a surplus of calories. Your body uses the surplus of calories to rebuild your strained muscles bigger than they were before the initial strain. To lose weight you must burn more calories than you eat. Some people are able to balance their training regimen to eat a surplus on days they lift weights and run a caloric deficit on days they do not work out. Most people (like us, unfortunately) try to do both and accomplish neither.

In our passage Paul tells us we can treasure Christ, or we can treasure other things, but we cannot treasure both. Only one goal can be our driving force. We either follow Christ or we don't.

1. Open today's study with a petition for eyes to see the treasures in God's Word. Ask Him to continue stirring your affections toward Him.

Uncover the Original Meaning

DECIDE which word you would like to study.

2. Write down any key words in Philippians 3:7–11 you'd like to study.

DISCOVER that word as it was originally written.

3. Using your preferred tool, discover the original word for *rubbish* in verse 8, and write it below.

DEFINE that word.

4. Fill out the following chart for the Greek word you found for *rubbish*.

GREEK WORD: VERSE AND VERSION:

Part of Speech: *(verb, noun, etc.)*	Translation Notes: *(How else is it translated? How often is this word used?)*
Strong's Concordance Number:	Definition:
Notes:	

5. Follow the Greek study steps to look up at least one more word in this week's passage. Here are a few you might start with:

surpassing worth (v. 8)

power (v. 10)

share (v. 10)

GREEK WORD: VERSE AND VERSION:

Part of Speech: (verb, noun, etc.)	Translation Notes: (How else is it translated? How often is this word used?)
Strong's Concordance Number:	Definition:
Notes:	

GREEK WORD:

VERSE AND VERSION:

Part of Speech: *(verb, noun, etc.)*	Translation Notes: *(How else is it translated? How often is this word used?)*
Strong's Concordance Number:	Definition:
Notes:	

Our hearts are so easily distracted. Though we know Christ is the only one who can fill the void in our souls, we give in to the temptation to try other things to bring us satisfaction. But those pursuits only leave us empty and thirsty. The presence of God alone can give us the living water that will quench our thirst.

{God, I want to know You more and more. Show me Your glory. Make my heart crave only You and Your will to be done in my life.}

IF YOU HAVE MORE TIME . . .

Clarification
Follow the Greek study steps for additional words in Philippians 3:7–11.

UTILIZATION

[FOCUSING ON PHILIPPIANS 3:7–11]

Now to the one who works, his wages are not counted as a gift but as his due. And to the one who does not work but believes in him who justifies the ungodly, his faith is counted as righteousness.

—Romans 4:4–5

IF YOU WERE to go to the bank and transfer money from your checking account into your savings account, two things would happen. First, your checking account would decrease. Second, your savings account would increase by the total your checking account decreased. One transfer requires two transactions.

This double transaction is what happens to people who trust Christ for salvation. First, our sins are placed on Jesus as He was on the Cross. Those sins were paid for and have been removed from us. Second, God credits to our account all the righteousness of Jesus. Since Jesus was perfectly righteous, we become the beneficiaries of His righteousness.

No one can ever earn righteousness. God's standard of righteousness is perfection, and we've already blown through that long ago. The only way we can ever become truly righteous is through faith. Part of our sinfulness is believing we can fix our sin problem on our own. Any attempt to clean ourselves up before God is actually a rejection of God's way of dealing with our sin. The only way to truly fix our sin problem is to stop trying to fix our sin problem and trust Jesus to pay what we owe. Only then does the double transaction occur—the debt of our sin for the righteousness of Christ.

1. Declare your need for God, once again. Confess the places you've been trying to fix your sin problem on your own. Thank God for the reality that you are already forgiven.

Discover the Connections

2. Read Philippians 3:7–11 to start your study today.

3. Look up each of the following references and record what you learn.

I counted as loss for the sake of Christ (v. 7)

       Hebrews 11:24–26

       1 Peter 4:14

have suffered the loss of all things and count them as rubbish (v. 8)

       Luke 9:25

righteousness from God that depends on faith (v. 9)

2 Corinthians 5:21

Paul truly understood the gospel—the good news about Jesus and His perfection given to undeserved sinners. Grace, grace, grace. Which undeserved sinners receive only by faith. Faith, faith, faith. The beginning of this great partnership we've been learning about starts with grace from God and the faith of man. Only grace. Only faith. And a soul-level understanding and acknowledgement of this great mystery is the spark that leads us to Christ and the fuel that continues to drive us to Christ. Our greatest treasure.

{God, I praise You for Your great, great grace. I am so thankful for the righteousness of Christ. I don't deserve it. I can't fully comprehend it. But I am grateful for it.}

IF YOU HAVE MORE TIME . . .

Utilization

Look up additional cross-references for words and/or phrases in this week's passage that you would like to learn more about.

power of His Resurrection (v. 10)

Romans 6:5–10

Colossians 2:12–14

Colossians 3:1

1 Thessalonians 5:9–10

SUMMATION

[FOCUSING ON PHILIPPIANS 3:7–11]

Because your steadfast love is better than life, my lips will praise you.

—Psalm 63:3

IMAGINE TWO WOMEN both on anniversary dates with their husbands. Wife number one has to remind her husband that it is, in fact, their anniversary. Her husband begrudgingly gets off the couch, puts on ratty, old sweatpants, and takes her to a restaurant. As he reads the menu, he complains about the price and orders the cheapest entree for the two of them. When signing for the bill, he looks at his wife and says, "Happy anniversary."

Wife number two receives a card on her nightstand the morning of her anniversary with an invitation to a date night. Her husband is dressed nicer than he was when he left for work. At dinner he effortlessly engages her in conversation about her day. When reading the menu he implores her to order the most expensive item. When she remarks about the cost, he explains that treating her is worth the cost. He doesn't bat an eye as he signs the check. Her husband looks at her and says, "Happy anniversary."

Which wife do you think feels more loved? Clearly, it is wife number two. Wife number one technically got a meal and an acknowledgement that it was her anniversary, but the begrudging attitude diminished the meaning of the acts.

In the same way, God doesn't want our begrudging love. He wants us to delight in Him. One of the most fundamental aspects of the Christian life is realizing true change doesn't come by trying our hardest; true change comes when our hearts desire something different. Our actions follow our affections. If we truly want to honor God, we will. If, though, we just want Jesus as an add-on to our lives, we will always struggle to grow.

Respond to God's Word

1. Declare your desire for more of God's presence. Ask Him for an ever growing longing to be satisfied by Him alone.

IDENTIFY—Find the main idea of each passage.

2. In the space provided, write out Philippians 3:7–11 in your own words.

3. Read a commentary or study Bible to see how your observations from this week line up with the scholars.

MODIFY—Evaluate my beliefs in light of the main idea.

Journal prayerfully through the following questions, asking the Spirit of God to enlighten and convict.

4. What do I primarily find my self-worth in?

5. What would I have a hard time letting go of and "counting all as loss" for the sake of knowing Christ better?

6. Am I primarily trying to walk with Christ out of duty or affection?

Obligatory Assignment   *Overflowing Affection*

GLORIFY—Align my life to reflect the truth of God's Word.

7. Brainstorm a few ways you can stir your affections for Christ this week. Consider reading and praying through Psalm 63, asking God to grant you a desperate heart for Him.

8. Pick one action and share it with a friend.

{Jesus, I do love You. Yet I have allowed the desires for earthly pleasures and the distractions of earthly pursuits keep me from living a life wholly devoted to You. Make my heart cry the same cry of Paul, to know You and love You and serve You above all.}

IF YOU HAVE MORE TIME . . .

Summation

Spend additional time in commentaries.

Add a title to this section in your outline in the appendix.

Pull out your journal and continue the conversation with God about what He is teaching you.

Share what you are learning with a trusted friend. Ask them to pray for you as you apply what you've learned.

WEEK 5: POINTS TO PONDER

[FOCUSING ON PHILIPPIANS 3:7–11]

True righteousness is not manmade.

THE REASON PAUL was able to walk away from his religious accomplishments was because he knew they could not produce the outcome he sought. God's standard for our righteousness is perfection. The thing about perfection is that it does not allow room for even one mistake. Perfection is not possible for humans; we are far too broken to even come close to God's standard. True righteousness is not living a good, moral life. True righteousness is not when our good outweighs our bad. True righteousness only comes through faith in Christ. God, in His mercy, did not leave us in our state of sinfulness but provided a means of escape. Because of the Cross, a double transaction can take place. Jesus took on all of our sin and we take on all of the righteousness He earned. This transaction does not happen because we live good lives; it is only applied to us if we come to Christ in faith. This does not mean we seek to live immoral lives. It means we understand our righteousness comes from Jesus, and in response to His righteousness we seek to follow the example He set.

Expect suffering.

Paul follows his statement about knowing Jesus and the power of His Resurrection by saying he wants to "share his sufferings, becoming like him in his death." If your pastor announced your church was going to start a sufferings ministry where you simply increased the amount of suffering in your life, how many of us would sign up? Most people will do anything they can to decrease the amount of suffering they experience in life, yet here is Paul, and he wants his suffering to increase. What is he talking about? Paul sandwiches this thought between two statements about resurrection. Jesus was raised from the dead (v. 10), Paul wants to experience resurrection (v. 11), and if he must suffer to gain this resurrection, so be it. This whole passage is about giving up lesser things in order to gain greater things. Is it really any wonder that Paul advocates giving up earthly comfort to gain eternal life, even if it costs him some suffering? We would do well to share this view. We live in a broken, sin-sick world where people get hurt and oppress others.

Jesus was persecuted, as were all of the apostles. If they experienced suffering for the faith we should expect to also.

Persist in the faith.

The biblical picture of the Christian life is that it is a life of persistent faith. Though by no means perfect, real followers of Christ will follow Christ for the rest of their lives. Unfortunately, many claim the name of Christ but do not really follow Him. This is what Jesus was denouncing in Matthew 7:22–23. Often a person will have some sort of religious experience at a service, camp, or retreat and make a decision for Christ. Having settled the issue of their eternal destiny they rarely, if ever, return to church and live a life indistinguishable from their lost neighbors.

Compare that brand of Christianity to Paul's words at the end of this section. He is not resting on the laurels of his Damascus Road experience, he is willing to do whatever it takes to get this resurrection from the dead. New Testament Christianity persists to the end. It never gives up, never turns aside, and is never satisfied with a past experience of Jesus.

CHEAT SHEET

Day 2: Observation

2. Let's take a deeper look at the cascade of desires recorded by Paul. Read Philippians 3:7–11, looking for the cause and effects in these verses. It may not be super clear at first glance. Pay attention to transition words such as *that*, *because*, and *for*.

Surpassing worth of knowing Christ ——→ Suffered the loss of all things/ counting them as rubbish ——→ Gain Christ and be found in Him ——→Possessing the righteousness of Christ through faith ——→ Know Him and the power of His Resurrection ——→ Share in His sufferings/ becoming like Him in His death ——→ Resurrection of the dead

Day 3: Clarification

4. Fill out the following chart for the Greek word you found for *rubbish*.

GREEK WORD:
skybalon

VERSE AND VERSION:
Philippians 3:8 ESV

Part of Speech: (verb, noun, etc.)	Translation Notes: (How else is it translated? How often is this word used?)
noun	*only used this one time*

Strong's Concordance Number:	Definition:
G4657	*refuse, garbage*

Notes:

To the degree that the Law is used in self-justification, it serves the flesh and is not just worthless but noxious and even abhorrent. The two elements in σκύβαλον, namely, worthlessness and filth, are best expressed by a term like "dung." [Gerhard Kittel, Geoffrey W. Bromiley, and Gerhard Friedrich, Theological Dictionary of the New Testament]

WEEK 6

FOCUSING ON PHILIPPIANS 4:4–9

God treated Jesus as we deserve—he took our penalty—so that, when we believe in him, God can treat us as Jesus deserved. More specifically, Jesus' prayers were given the rejection that we sinners merit so that our prayers could have the reception that he merits.

—TIM KELLER, *PRAYER*

LAST SUMMER, WE took the kids to Chicago. One of the must-do activities in the Windy City is going to the Sky Deck at Willis Tower (formerly known as the Sears Tower). From the 103rd floor you can step into a glass case and look straight down, over a thousand feet, to the city streets below. Many who step into the case are fearful of taking a peek until they have spent a few moments in the chamber.

In a similar way, many action movies require a character, usually the main character, to travel to dizzying heights. At the top floor of a high-rise tower, the edge of a cliff, the door of an airplane, or the apex of a bridge, the character will be forced to deal with the specter of falling from a great height. Usually in this moment the main character will say to themselves, "Don't look down!"

Whether it is from a glass window case above a Midwestern city or a rope in an action flick we instinctively tell ourselves not to look down. This is probably because we know if we do look down there is a high likelihood that fear will take the reins, making it that much harder to focus on the task at hand—whether that may be to save the free world or snap that family photo.

These moments demonstrate the power of our thought life. Focusing on the height only makes it less likely to find safety. In the same way, if we continually focus on the things that bring us fear, anxiety, and worry, we will gravitate toward those emotions and live like there is no alternative. If, however, we continually preach to ourselves that God is bigger than any circumstance, we will be reminded that He is in control.

This is not simply keeping a positive mental attitude. This is actively guarding that which we choose to believe. If we are convinced that God is who He says He is in Scripture, we must allow these beliefs to shape our thought life.

In our passage this week, Paul is exhorting the church at Philippi to stop worrying and start praying. He continues by giving them better things to think about: that which is true, honorable, just, lovely, commendable, excellent, and worthy of praise. As you study, we pray your heart is stirred toward a default of prayer in every circumstance.

FOUNDATION

[FOCUSING ON PHILIPPIANS 4:4–9]

For this I toil, struggling with all his energy that he powerfully works within me.

—Colossians 1:29

BEFORE THE INVENTION of modern irrigation systems, farmers were solely dependent upon rain to water their crops. If the rain did not come, the crops would not grow. Many times in the Old Testament, famine occurred and almost always because of a drought. Even in our recent history, much of the American Great Plains were hit hard by the Dust Bowl in the 1930s.

In order for crops to grow, though, it requires more than just rain. To produce a harvest, the farmer must work the soil, plant the seeds, and keep pests away. Sometimes a farmer does this work and the rain doesn't come. However, if the farmer does not plant the seeds, no amount of rain will bring a harvest. As Christians we understand God sends the rain, so every crop is a partnership between God and the farmer.

This partnership is the portrait Paul continues to paint for us. God answers our prayers—and gives us peace that passes understanding—but we still must faithfully bring our requests to Him. It is a mistake to believe God plays no part in our lives, but it is also a mistake to believe we play no part. Failure to pray and obey is like a farmer who doubts the rain will come, so he never plants any seeds.

1. Before we dive into Philippians 4:4–9, spend a moment in prayer. Ask God to open your eyes to the life-changing truths in this passage.

Enjoy Every Word

2. Once again, for our Foundation day, we'll work through the first layer of this week's section of Philippians 4:4–9. Write out the passage in the space provided.

3. Which words or phrases in Philippians 4:4–9 stand out to you?

4. Record any questions you have about this passage.

These things. Think about them. Practice them. And the God of peace will be with you. The God who holds all things in His sustaining care is always with us. But when we mute our ears to the truth He speaks and instead allow our thought-life to be filled with the what-ifs and the why-nots, we forfeit the peace that comes with His presence.

{Once again, Lord, I am thankful for Your power working within me. Grant me the energy and focus to work diligently on the tasks You've given me. Make me sure of my calling and relentless in my pursuit of it. As I follow You in obedience, make me mute to the lies of the evil one. Keep my mind steadfast on You—Your glorious character and good plan.}

IF YOU HAVE MORE TIME . . .

Foundation

Write out Philippians 4:4–9 onto a few 3-by-5 cards in your favorite translation. Keep the verses with you and/or post them around your house, and commit them to memory.

OBSERVATION

[FOCUSING ON PHILIPPIANS 4:4–9]

You keep him in perfect peace whose mind is stayed on you, because he trusts in you.

—Isaiah 26:3

NEITHER OF US are what you'd call neat freaks. Katie has a streak of orderliness buried deep down inside of her, but the years of messy motherhood has forced her to push those urges down. There are, however, a few spaces in our lives we must keep clean out of necessity. One is the windshields of our cars. It's important to keep them clean and clear so we can see the road while we drive. The guts of a freshly smacked insect right in front of our line of sight are not something that can be ignored.

Thank goodness for windshield wipers and washer fluid, or we'd all be in trouble. Without them, our view would be cluttered with bugs commanding our undivided attention. Yet, even with the wipers, these bugs can become a problem if we fixate on them. Trying to get every last remnant of the bug off—while still driving—might cause us to run off the road or run into something. Focusing on the windshield draws attention from the road. How embarrassing would it be to explain to the police officer that we totaled our car because we were worried about bugs on the windshield?

Of course, it is silly to focus on the windshield when the greater responsibility is to focus on the road ahead. This is exactly what we do when we worry. We focus on the problem in front of us, rather than the big picture: God is in control. He has a plan. We can trust Him.

1. Open your time with God with a declaration of who He is. Regardless of how you feel, let your thoughts be fixed on the powerful, able, and faithful character of God.

Look at the Details

2. As you head back to Philippians 4:4–9, look for commands and record them in the space provided.

3. Read Philippians 4:4–9 one more time and look for promises.

Only God brings calm into our chaos. God alone can provide peace to our soul. Our job is not to control our situation or fret over what is or is not. The work ahead of us is to continually present our requests to our capable God and rest in the fact that He knows and sees and always delivers. (For a deeper study of this passage and our experience of God's promised peace, pick up Katie's *Everyday Peace* Bible study.)

{*God, I confess I all too often fixate on the problems right in front of me instead of fixing my gaze on Your goodness. You promise to guard me with Your peace. I cling to You as my only hope, my capable provider, and my faithful rescuer.*}

IF YOU HAVE MORE TIME . . .

Observation

Note all that is true about the peace of God in these verses.

CLARIFICATION

[FOCUSING ON PHILIPPIANS 4:4–9]

But the wisdom from above is first pure, then peaceable, gentle, open to reason, full of mercy and good fruits, impartial and sincere.

—James 3:17

WHEN OUR KIDS were babies they cried; it was the strangest thing. Whenever they got hungry, tired, or in need of a diaper change, they would just wail until we did something to fix the situation. No amount of logic or reason seemed to work with them. Try as we might to explain the factors to them, it was all to no avail.

Obviously, this is satire. Babies are not known for their reasonableness. Yet, as our children grew, they became more rational. It is the expected development of a child to become less self-centered and demanding. As Christians, we too should continually grow in maturity, becoming more and more known as those who are no longer infants but mature, selfless, and reasonable Christ-followers.

1. Ask God to help you as you dive into the Greek today. Thank Him for His precious, perfect Word.

Uncover the Original Meaning

DECIDE which word you would like to study.

2. Look for any potential key words in Philippians 4:4–9. As you find any repeated word or words that seem important to the passage, write them in the space provided.

DISCOVER that word as it was originally written.

3. Discover the original word for *reasonable* in verse 5, and write it below.

DEFINE that word.

4. Fill out the chart for the Greek word you found for *reasonable*.

GREEK WORD: VERSE AND VERSION:

Part of Speech: *(verb, noun, etc.)*	Translation Notes: *(How else is it translated? How often is this word used?)*
Strong's Concordance Number:	Definition:
Notes:	

5. Follow the Greek study steps to look up at least one more word in this week's passage. Here are a few you might start with:

rejoice (v. 4)

guard (v. 7)

think about (v. 8)

GREEK WORD: VERSE AND VERSION:

Part of Speech:
(verb, noun, etc.)

Translation Notes:
(How else is it translated? How often is this word used?)

Strong's Concordance Number:

Definition:

Notes:

GREEK WORD:

VERSE AND VERSION:

Part of Speech:
(verb, noun, etc.)

Translation Notes:
(How else is it translated? How often is this word used?)

Strong's Concordance Number:

Definition:

Notes:

The way we act ought to be fitting with our identity as a Christ-follower—gentle, generous, and considerate like Christ. Yet Christians are often known as unreasonable and unkind. In our efforts to stand uncompromisingly on the standards of God's moral standards, we often communicate an air of superiority and intolerance toward others. Yes, we must hold unswervingly to God's call to holiness, but we must not forget to love the souls bound by sin.

{Jesus, I am thankful for Your perfect example of how to balance truth with grace toward those who embrace the sin-filled lifestyle. Grant me a soft heart toward those who act and think differently from me. May Your gentle, generous character be made known to those around me and give me opportunities to lovingly tell them of Your truth.}

IF YOU HAVE MORE TIME . . .

Clarification

Follow the Greek study steps for additional words in Philippians 4:4–9.

UTILIZATION

[FOCUSING ON PHILIPPIANS 4:4–9]

*We must work the works of him who sent me while
it is day; night is coming, when no one can work.*
—John 9:4

BOTH OF OUR drivers' licenses have designations to show we've chosen to be organ donors. We both agree that once our spirits leave this earth, we want our bodies to be used in whatever way they can to provide rescue to those in need. However, our organs will only be useful to save lives if they get to the recipients in time. Human tissue is only viable for a few precious hours, after which it becomes useless. But unlike human tissue, the message of the gospel is timeless and can always bring life and rescue to a soul that needs it.

Even though Paul taught extensively about the sovereignty of God, he lived with an undying urgency to share the gospel with the lost. He couples his command to be reasonable to everyone with "the Lord is at hand." With great urgency, this ticking eternal clock drove Paul to go from town to town preaching the good news, organizing new believers into churches, and remaining willing to pay whatever price necessary for the success of the mission.

1. Pray for an urgency like Paul's. Ask the Holy Spirit to open your eyes to the lostness around you. Commit to God anew to preach the gospel whatever the cost.

Discover the Connections

2. Read Philippians 4:4–9 to start your study today.

3. Study each set of verses and take notes of any enlightening truths.

The Lord is at hand

1 Peter 4:7

Romans 10:14–15

Romans 13:11–12

Hebrews 10:24–25

Souls are eternal and are lost and dying every day. If I'm (Katie) honest, this truth does not sear my heart the way it should. I do not always take the role of ambassador for Christ seriously. I do not live a life of urgency.

{Lord, help me. Burn a fire in my soul for those who do not know You. Make me more fervent in prayer, aware of the people in my life who need You, and active in sharing the good news with them. Have mercy on me for my lack of urgency for the lost state of so many.}

IF YOU HAVE MORE TIME . . .

Utilization

Look up additional cross-references for words and/ or phrases in this week's passage that you would like to learn more about.

do not be anxious about anything (v. 6)

Matthew 6:25–34

1 Peter 5:6–7

the peace of God (v. 7)

Isaiah 26:3

John 14:27

Colossians 3:15

SUMMATION

[FOCUSING ON PHILIPPIANS 4:4–9]

Peace I leave with you; my peace I give to you. Not as the world gives do I give to you. Let not your hearts be troubled, neither let them be afraid.

—John 14:27

LAST YEAR I (Katie) had an odd infection in the back of one my fingers. It was extremely painful and quickly became red and swollen. I was fairly sure it was a festering staph infection, and I knew the over-the-counter ointment I had in my medicine cabinet was not going to cut it. I made an appointment with my family doctor, and she brought relief to the wound by lancing the infection and giving me a prescription for an antibiotic. Within a few days the finger had reduced in swelling, but I could tell the infection was still present. I had planned to call the doctor's office that afternoon, but they beat me to it. The wound culture and antibiotic susceptibility test came back, and the bug in my appendage was not going to be killed off with the drugs I was taking. A new, more powerful prescription was called in, and within days there was no sign of the superbug.

The spread of antibiotic-resistant bacteria is reaching epidemic proportions. Doctors believe the reason for this spread is patients not finishing their prescribed medication once they begin feeling better. Even though our physicians have spent years of their lives—and hundreds of thousands of dollars—to become doctors, many patients believe themselves to be smarter than their doctor when it comes to medication.

We have a tendency to treat our spiritual sicknesses this way as well. We know what God's Word tells us about our ailments, but we think we can figure things out on our own. Prescribe our own treatment plan. This week's passage gives us the cure for worry: prayer. The command to not be anxious is conjoined with the command to let your request be made known to God. These commands are one in the same. Yet, we think we are smarter than Scripture and try to medicate worry on our own. The result is anxiety run rampant.

Respond to God's Word

1. Spend time listing your anxieties. Prayerfully ask God to reveal any places of worry, doubt, fear, and anxiety you might be hiding.

IDENTIFY—Find the main idea of each passage.

2. Take a few moments to flip back to each day's study to review what you've learned this week. In the space provided, write out Philippians 4:4–9 in your own words. Or simply write out what you think the main idea of this passage is.

3. Check out a commentary or your study Bible to see how your observations from this week line up.

MODIFY—Evaluate my beliefs in light of the main idea.

Journal prayerfully through the following questions, asking the Spirit of God to enlighten and convict.

4. What is my experience of God's promised peace?

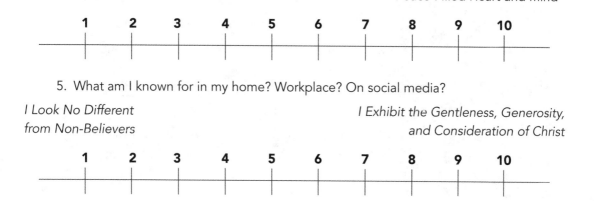

No Peace at All   Peace-Filled Heart and Mind

1   2   3   4   5   6   7   8   9   10

5. What am I known for in my home? Workplace? On social media?

I Look No Different from Non-Believers   I Exhibit the Gentleness, Generosity, and Consideration of Christ

1   2   3   4   5   6   7   8   9   10

6. What level of urgency do I have for God's name and grace to be known among the lost?

Lack of Urgency　　　　　　　　　　　　　　　　　　　　　　*Consuming Fervency*

1　2　3　4　5　6　7　8　9　10

GLORIFY—Align my life to reflect the truth of God's Word.

7. What is God speaking to my heart this week? What actions do I need to take moving forward?

{God, I can easily become overwhelmed with how far away my heart and life are from Your purpose and plan for me. Give me one specific action to take today and the grace and strength to carry it out. I long to live a life as Your faithful servant.}

IF YOU HAVE MORE TIME . . .

Summation

Spend additional time in commentaries.

Add a title to this section in your outline in the appendix.

Pull out your journal and continue the conversation with God about what He is teaching you.

Share what you are learning with a trusted friend. Ask them to pray for you as you apply what you've learned.

WEEK 6: POINTS TO PONDER

[FOCUSING ON PHILIPPIANS 4:4–9]

Rejoice in every circumstance.

EVEN IN THE midst of this painful personal struggle, Paul chooses to rejoice and invites the church to do so as well. If you look at the words Paul uses, it is verbal overkill. In verse 4 he says, "Rejoice . . . always; again I will say, rejoice." He really cannot fathom a situation in which he would fail to rejoice.

The Christian life is a call to rejoice always in all circumstances. Of course, there are many times in life when rejoicing is not the first thing that comes to mind. These times include the loss of a loved one, ending of a relationship, loss of a job, or an ominous diagnosis. The list could go on and on. You may be thinking, *How are we to rejoice in the midst of circumstances like that?* Remember where Paul is—in prison for his faith. He is awaiting trial in Rome, the same government who crucified Jesus. Ultimately Paul was killed by the Roman government for his faith. Even in the midst of that, Paul says *rejoice.*

Perhaps it is helpful to look at where Paul says the rejoicing takes place, "Rejoice in the Lord." We are not called to rejoice that we have pain, sorrow, and suffering. Nor are we supposed to rejoice in the power of the human spirit or positive thinking. Christians rejoice in the Lord. Such rejoicing can only take place within the framework of our connection to God. We are to rejoice that a holy God would accept guilty sinners into His family. We should rejoice that a faithful God will not cast us out if we come to Him in faith. We rejoice that a loving God knows our sorrows and cares deeply for us. We can rejoice that a sovereign God is working all of this pain and suffering not for our harm but for our good. We rejoice knowing that an eternal God will one day bring an end to all suffering and pain. Even in the midst of our deepest hurts, we can still rejoice if we rejoice in the Lord.

Be gentle in every circumstance.

In verse 5, Paul says we are to let our "reasonableness be known to everyone." You probably discovered this word *reasonableness* can also be translated as *gentleness.* Both present the concept that we are not to be harsh or abusive to others for any reason.

How do you respond to people in the midst of conflict? Are you reasonable and gentle or combative and vindictive? Many people can seem warm and friendly when there is no conflict. The minute you cross them, though, a switch flips, and they reveal a side never before seen. If this describes you perhaps you need to rest in the knowledge that God fights your battles much better than you do. Rather than rushing toward a fight, rejoice and pray.

Pray in every circumstance.

In verses 6–7 Paul established a contrast between anxiety and prayer. In Paul's mind these two cannot coexist. If we are anxious, the solution is prayer. As we pray we find relief from anxiety. As we pray we receive the peace of God.

Paul wants the church to know there is a correlation between their view of God and anxiety. If we believe in a small God our problems will seem big; if we believe in a big God our problems will seem small and insignificant. The connection between anxiety, prayer, and peace is found in the character of God. If we really trust that God is sovereign, we know He is in control even when we feel out of control. If we believe God is good, we can rest in the knowledge that His plans for us are good, even better than ones we would come up with.

When we bring our concerns to a good, sovereign God, we can be sure He has heard them and will respond perfectly to them. The result of this process is peace. The only way we lose this peace is by neglecting prayer and focusing on our problems.

Maintain a healthy thought life.

Many armchair psychologists have instructed others to think happy thoughts. It is perhaps more helpful for us to think *healthy* thoughts. This does not mean we visualize yoga poses and sunsets. Paul's instruction for the church at Philippi was to commit to thinking good things, or as he says, "what ever is just . . . pure . . . lovely . . . commendable . . . any excellence . . . anything worthy of praise, think about these things" (v. 8).

It is not by mistake that Paul places this directive after his instruction about anxiety and prayer. If we want to maintain our freedom from anxiety we must police our own thoughts. It will not be surprising that we fall back into fear when we think about everything that is wrong or could go wrong in the world—especially while living at the confluence of the 24-hour news cycle and social media.

Until about 100 years ago, news came once a day with the morning newspaper. The advent of radio, then television, made news more accessible, but news was relegated to nightly updates. Cable news networks created platforms not only to report on news all day but comment on it as well. This ushered in the era of the 24-hour news cycle. Now that most people have cameras on their phones, a social media network, and global internet access, no event goes unreported. The net effect of this confluence is there are more things than ever to worry about.

In addition to prayer we must also combat these influences with a healthy thought life. This may mean turning off the television, leaving the phone alone, and unpluging from the constant flow of information.

WEEK 6: CHEAT SHEET

Day 2: Observation

2. As you head back to Philippians 4:4–9, look for commands.

   Rejoice

   Rejoice

   Let your reasonableness be known to everyone

   Do not be anxious

   Let your requests be made known to God

   Think about "these things" (whatever is . . .)

   Practice "these things" (what you've learned, received, heard, and seen from Paul)

3. Read Philippians 4:4–9 one more time and look for promises

   The peace of God will guard my heart and mind

   The God of peace will be with me

Day 3: Clarification

4. Fill out the chart for the Greek word you found for *reasonable*.

GREEK WORD:

epieikēs

VERSE AND VERSION:

Philippians 4:5 ESV

Part of Speech:
(verb, noun, etc.)

adjective

Translation Notes:
(How else is it translated? How often is this word used?)

used 5 times; all other occurrences translated as gentle

Strong's Concordance Number:

G1933

Definition:

fitting; fair; meet; good

Notes:

So I suggest translating the neuter adjective **epieikēs** *used substantivally as "friendly equilibrium" in Phil 4:5, where the Vulgate uses the word* **modestia**: *"Let your friendly, well-balanced character be known to all." This favorable reputation and especially this attractiveness are self-evident. [Ceslas Spicq and James D. Ernest, Theological Lexicon of the New Testament]*

CLOSING THOUGHTS

What a journey. The Book of Philippians is filled to the brim with foundational truths, precious promises, and realigning commands. We have both studied through this book numerous times, and each walk through these pages leads us to deeper, more glorious truths about our Savior and His heart for us. We pray your study has been a fruitful one. We're also asking that the Holy Spirit would continue His work in your heart and mind to conform you more and more into the image of Christ as you work our your salvation daily.

Our hope is you've not only grown in your love for God's Word over these last several weeks but that you also feel more equipped to study the Bible on your own after using this study guide. His Word is alive and active, overflowing with the life-giving declarations of our Rescuer and His good plan for us. We pray your grasp on His Word grows ever tighter, your view of God continually increases, and your desire for the presence of Christ swells greater each day as you learn to better engage with Him in this holy partnership of your sanctification.

Thanks for taking this journey with us.

– Chris and Katie Orr

BONUS STUDY WEEKS

BONUS WEEK A
FOCUSING ON PHILIPPIANS 1:1–5

IF YOU WERE to go through your contact list in your phone or on social media, you would probably be able to group these people into categories. Some would be associates at work, acquaintances whom you've long since lost touch with, or the plumber you called when the upstairs bath leaked onto the dining room table. Others may be family members scattered across the nation or world. The rest are probably your friends.

Your friends could be further categorized as well. Some friends you only see once or twice a year. Some friends might be a part of your everyday routine. But no matter who you are or what your station in life, we all have those friends who wear us out. You see that name pop up on caller ID and you shiver. You know they are going to be a drain on your time, attention, or emotions. Sure, you love them, but the relationship is very taxing. They need you to be a shoulder to cry on, a problem solver, an ATM, or a taxi service. However they come, their presence is an invasion of your life. If you don't have any friends who fit into this category there is the distinct possibility you are that friend. If so, not to worry; God's grace abounds. You can learn how to be a better friend.

The relationship Paul had with most churches he wrote fit in this last category. Nearly all his letters are written to correct some problem or settle some crisis.

There is one more group of friends we haven't mentioned—great friends. Those friends are a breath of fresh air. Spending time with them is no chore. In fact, time flies when you are with them. This is the type of relationship Paul has with the church at Philippi. The letter he sends them contains no corrections or rebukes, only encouragement.

As you study this week, notice the love Paul has for this particular church. We pray God would give you this kind of love for a specific local church. If you already have this kind of love for your church, pray for it as you begin this week's study.

Foundation

Read and copy Philippians 1:1–5.

Observation

Note all you can learn about Paul in these verses.

Clarification

- ▪ **DECIDE:** Look for potential key words in Philippians 1:1–5.
- ▪ **DISCOVER:** Choose a word to look up to find its original Greek word.
- ▪ **DEFINE:** Fill out a Greek study chart to learn more about that word. *You can find blank Greek charts at KatieOrr.me/Resources.*

Utilization

Follow the cross-references in this week's passage. Here are a few to start with:

overseers (v. 1)

1 Timothy 3:1–7

deacons (v. 1)

1 Timothy 3:8–13

Summation

- ▪ **IDENTIFY**—Find the main idea of this passage. Consult commentaries to check your conclusions.
- ▪ **MODIFY**—Evaluate my beliefs in light of the main idea. Is there anything I need to change in my beliefs because of what I've studied this week?
- ▪ **GLORIFY**—Align my life to reflect the truth of God's Word. What is God leading me to do as a result of this week's study?

POINTS TO PONDER

You don't love Christ if you don't love the church.

Paul was writing to a specific church: the church at Philippi. Paul begins this letter by talking about his appreciation for this church. It has become fashionable in our day to embrace Christianity but reject the church. We believe this is a foolish notion that would be foreign to Paul and the rest of the New Testament authors. To claim to love Christ but hate His bride (Ephesians 5:25–32) is similar to saying you want to be an NBA player but don't want to be on any NBA teams. No church is perfect, but you will not find any passage of Scripture that tells you to stay away from church until you find the perfect one. In fact, you will find quite the opposite. If you are doing this study but are not plugged into a local church, we encourage you to find a church to worship with this week.

Pray for your church.

In verse three Paul mentions his frequent prayers for this church. Paul was the one who planted this church, but he could not stay with them very long. Like a concerned parent, Paul desires their success and health. He is unable to be there in person, so the only thing left to do is pray. In addition to being a member of a local church and being plugged into the life of that church, we are also encouraged to pray for our church. There is no shortage of things to pray about for your church.

BONUS WEEK B
FOCUSING ON PHILIPPIANS 1:12–19

IF YOU HAVE watched the Discovery Channel in recent years you may have noticed the surge in shows that focus on life in Alaska. One of this network's biggest hits is *Deadliest Catch*, a show about crab fishing in the Bering Sea. The show chronicles the Herculean efforts of captains and crews to get crab from the sea floor to the grocery store.

Like many forms of commercial fishing, crab fishing is a highly regulated industry that only operates seasonally. Ships featured on the show fish for king crab in the fall and snow crab in the winter. The reason many find the show so compelling is that the Bering Sea in the dead of winter is one of the most treacherous waterways in the entire world. Captains often spend entire seasons dodging hurricane force winds and crippling ice. Given the short window they have to catch these tasty sea creatures, crewmen work up to 36 hours at a time without rest.

The reason the show is titled *Deadliest Catch* is because far too many fishermen have lost their lives in this fishery. There is no shortage of ways to suffer death or injury on a crab fishing boat. Crab pots weigh about a ton and have crushed deckhands, leaving them maimed or dead. Thousands of feet of rope go over the rail of the boat, and one wrong step can cause a foot to get tangled in a rope headed straight to the bottom of the sea. Additionally, rogue waves as tall as skyscrapers can capsize a boat in a heartbeat.

Captains and crew who are willing to brave these risks and successfully navigate the dangers are paid handsomely for their efforts. Since it is common for deckhands aboard these ships to get paid a year's worthy of salary for a few months' worth of work, the show always has greenhorns—first year crewmen. Most of the greenhorns leave crab fishing after one or two seasons, unable or unwilling to cope with the rigors of the fishery. Those who survive their greenhorn years are the ones who are willing to do whatever it takes to get the job done.

Though separated by a couple of millennia, Paul would have related to the guys in this hit show. Paul exhibited a similar willingness to do whatever it takes to get the job done. As you study our passage this week, we pray that God would give you this kind of resolve in His kingdom.

Foundation

Read and copy Philippians 1:12–19.

Observation

Read Philippians 1:12–19, and look for the two groups of people Paul refers to. Using the information we have in verses 15–17, list characteristics for each group.

Read Philippians 1:12–19 again, looking for the two factors Paul mentions will bring his deliverance.

Clarification

- **DECIDE:** Look for potential key words in Philippians 1:12–19.
- **DISCOVER:** Choose a word to look up to find its original Greek word.
- **DEFINE:** Fill out a Greek study chart to learn more about that word.

Utilization

Follow the cross-references in this week's passage. Here are a few to start with:

speak the Word without fear (v. 14)

Acts 4:31

knowing that I am put here (v. 16)

1 Corinthians 9:16–19

Summation

- **IDENTIFY**—Find the main idea of this passage.
  Consult commentaries to double check your conclusions.
- **MODIFY**—Evaluate my beliefs in light of the main idea.
  Do I tend to think more about the here and now or all that is to come?
  What trials and/or frustrating people are heavy on my heart today?
- **GLORIFY**—Align my life to reflect the truth of God's Word.
  What is God leading me to do as a result of this week's study?

POINTS TO PONDER

Do whatever it takes to make the gospel known.

Paul is writing to the church in Philippi from prison. Most people would take this opportunity to throw a pity party and invite everyone they know. Paul, however, understands God is using his imprisonment to advance the kingdom. Paul gives two ways his imprisonment is helping the cause of Christ. First, he is given the chance to minister to the guards. Second, other Christians have seen Paul's boldness and taken heart. Rather than focusing on his circumstances, Paul looks to the work of God and is excited. This kind of excitement only comes when we are willing to do whatever it takes to make the gospel known. Paul was willing to go to prison if it helped the cause.

Value people more than your preferences.

We can be certain that—all things being equal—Paul would have preferred to be free rather than in prison. It's not that Paul has a particular affinity for prison culture, he simply had a higher preference than his own freedom. Paul valued the work of the gospel more than he valued his preference for freedom. One of the most insidious ways Satan corrupts the witness of a local church is by convincing its members to value their own preferences over other people. The minute we view church as a vehicle for our entertainment rather than an organization for God's glory, we miss the point. The church is designed to be a battleship, not a cruise ship. Cruise ships are a great way to relax and unwind. They often have unending arrays of food, a plethora of activities for all ages, excursions for the more adventurous ones, and an attentive staff who cater to every whim of those aboard. Many people have this same view of the local church. It is more fitting to view the church, though, as a battleship. Battleships are built to engage the enemy, turn back evil, and advance the cause of good. Those aboard battleships know the vessel's primary purpose is not their amusement or comfort but rather the success of the mission. By thinking more like sailors and less like vacationers, we too can exhibit the mindset of Paul.

Pursue gospel clarity.

Paul is so focused on making the gospel known that he rejoices—even when people do it the wrong way. Make no mistake, had they messed with the message, Paul would have been the first to correct and rebuke them. The issue in this passage, however, is not that they are preaching the wrong gospel, but that they preach the gospel with wrong motives. It is safe to assume Paul's first choice would be for everyone to preach the true gospel with a true heart. In the absence of that option, Paul will settle for the true gospel being preached with selfish motives. This sounds like a strange concession, but we should be glad Paul made it.

How often do you hear of preachers or church staff who sin in a very public fashion? More often than any of us would like to admit. If Paul advocated that wrong motivations negated the message of the gospel, then everyone who followed that erring pastor would be forced to question their faith. If we really drill down deep, how many people can say every decision they have ever made in ministry was made out of completely pure motives? By placing the importance on the gospel message, not the purity of the messenger, Paul comforts those who find themselves in such situations.

BONUS WEEK C
FOCUSING ON PHILIPPIANS 1:27–30

I (CHRIS) SPENT about three years as a youth pastor for 6th–12th grade students. This particular church had a large, blue, 22-passenger bus we would use for trips. Since the bus was so long, it came with an internal public address system the driver could use to communicate with the passengers. It was my custom every time I took the students out on that bus to pick up the radio and remind them of one simple rule: "Don't be an idiot." While it may seem harsh to some of you, I assure you this one simple rule covers a multitude of foolish behaviors. Often when you get kids in this age together in groups and away from their parents, they will make decisions they would never make with mom or dad around. A simple reminder was always necessary when we ventured off church grounds.

One of the main reasons it was always necessary to remind the kids of this rule was that when you arrive in a giant blue bus people take notice. Every time we went into a movie theater, skating rink, or mini golf course people were watching our behavior more closely than they were the kids who showed up in a nondescript sedan.

Often our students would bring their unbelieving friends on these trips who had never stepped foot into church on a Sunday morning. Of course, it would be impossible for anyone at a skating rink to know which kids were "church kids" and which were not. Whether it was right or fair, every second we spent in these establishments we were representing that church, and by extension Christ Himself. If we left the place a mess or were rude to the staff they would surely notice. How many people in the service industry have been turned off to Christ after serving Christians?

You may not arrive to work in a big blue bus, but if you claim the name of Christ people are watching you. Everything you do is a reflection of Christ. This week we will see Paul encouraging the church to live in a way that is worthy of the gospel. In fact, this is actually the first command in Paul's letter to the church at Philippi. Paul knew this one command would cover a multitude of behaviors.

We pray you'll find a new resolve to live worthy of the gospel after this week's study.

Foundation

Read and copy Philippians 1:27–30

Observation

Note all that Paul hopes is true of the church at Philippi.

What does Paul say has been granted to the church?

Clarification

- **DECIDE:** Look for potential key words in Philippians 1:27–30.
- **DISCOVER:** Choose a word to look up to find its original Greek word.
- **DEFINE:** Fill out a Greek study chart to learn more about that word.

Utilization

Follow the cross-references in this week's passage. Here are a few to start with:

conflict (v. 30)

Colossians 1:29

1 Timothy 6:12

2 Timothy 4:7

you saw I had (v. 30)

Acts 16:19–40

1 Thessalonians 2:2

Summation

- **IDENTIFY**—Find the main idea of this passage.
  Consult commentaries to double check your conclusions.
- **MODIFY**—Evaluate my beliefs in light of the main idea.
  What is my experience of the local church? Am I standing firm with them in one spirit? Striving side-by-side with them for the faith of the gospel?
  Verse 29 tells us that suffering is granted for the sake of Christ. How does this perspective compare to my first reaction when difficulties come?

How would I categorize my current way of life?

*An Offense to
the Gospel*

*Worthy Reflection
of the Gospel*

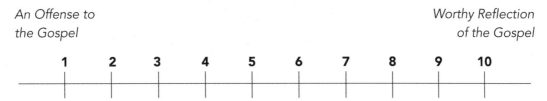

- **GLORIFY**—Align my life to reflect the truth of God's Word.
What is God leading me to do as a result of this week's study?

POINTS TO PONDER

Live worthy of the gospel.

It is important to distinguish that Paul is not commanding us to live lives worthy of forgiveness—we won't ever be worthy of God's love or acceptance. Rather, Paul's encouragement is to live a life worthy of the gospel. Living worthy of forgiveness is saying we can earn our salvation by becoming worthy of it. Living worthy of the gospel is something that can only happen after salvation as a response to it.

Stand firm against opposition.

In verse 28, Paul encourages the church to resist fearing their opponents. Anyone can lash out in anger, but Christians are to stand firm in faith. As we maintain our unity and fearlessness in the midst of struggle, our enemies will be able to see their hostility is not right. They can either continue to hate God and march to their own destruction or repent and join us. In either case, it is not our position to return hostility for hostility.

Don't expect life to be easy.

Paul concludes chapter 1 with a word of encouragement about suffering. Paul says suffering is granted to us. We may tend to think, *Gee thanks, God, but I think I will pass.* By suffering, Paul views Christians as joining Christ in every way. Jesus suffered. Paul suffered in the past and was presently suffering. Therefore, the Philippian church should not fear their present sufferings either.

BONUS WEEK D
FOCUSING ON PHILIPPIANS 2:9–11

RECENTLY, THE HIGH school in our town experienced athletic success when the girls' basketball team won the state championship. In case you weren't aware, basketball is a big deal in Kentucky, so it was a massive accomplishment for these girls to win the school's first state championship. At the end of the game a stage was brought out to center court for the team to stand on as they took pictures with the championship trophy. The stage was also used by the losing team as they held their runner-up trophy. The scene was a picture of polar opposites. One team was celebrating while shedding tears of joy while the other was inconsolable, crying tears of agony. At the end of the game there was no doubt who the winner was, but this truth elicited very different responses depending on which team you were on.

This polarity is what Paul is describing in the passage this week. Currently, there are some who proclaim Jesus as the reigning King. However, there are many, billions in fact, who do not believe Jesus to be King. There will be a day, though, when no one will question the kingship and authority of Jesus. Paul says, "Every knee should bow . . . and every tongue confess that Jesus Christ is Lord" (vv. 10–11). On that day those who trust Christ for salvation will say this willingly and with great joy. Those who reject Jesus will also acknowledge His title of King, but they will not love His rule. Not a single soul in hell will be confused as to who the rightful King is, but this is not to say they welcome Jesus' reign.

Foundation

Read and copy Philippians 2:9–11.

Observation

Looking at verse 9, record all the actions God took because of Christ's obedience.

Clarification

■ **DECIDE:** Look for potential key words in Philippians 2:9–11.

■ **DISCOVER:** Choose a word to look up to find its original Greek word.

■ **DEFINE:** Fill out a Greek study chart to learn more about that word.

Utilization

Follow the cross-references in this week's passage. Here are a few to start with:

every tongue confess (v. 11)

Matthew 10:32

Romans 10:9

in heaven and on earth and under the earth (v. 10)

Ephesians 1:7–10

Colossians 1:16

Summation

- ▢ **IDENTIFY**—Find the main idea of this passage.
  Consult commentaries to double check your conclusions.
- ▢ **MODIFY**—Evaluate my beliefs in light of the main idea.
  How often do I praise Jesus for who He is?
  Do I truly believe Jesus Christ is Lord of all?
  Do I eagerly anticipate the day that every knee will bow to Christ our Lord?
- ▢ **GLORIFY**—Align my life to reflect the truth of God's Word.
  What is God leading me to do as a result of this week's study?

POINTS TO PONDER

Jesus is now the exalted king.

Jesus humbled Himself having come to earth and walked around in our shoes for more than thirty years. After dying on the Cross, Jesus was raised from the dead, defeating sin, death, and hell. Upon His Resurrection, Jesus' time of humility was over. Now He is the exalted one. Jesus sits at the right hand of the Father, the place of favor. All who come to Jesus in faith worship Him as Lord of their lives. Though we exist under human rulers and authorities there is only one king for believers: King Jesus. However, not everyone on earth knows about Jesus. In many corners of the globe there are people who have never even heard His name. In other places people have heard the name but deny Him honor.

Jesus will one day be the undisputed King.

Paul tells us there is a day coming when Jesus will be recognized as King by everyone everywhere. At present, Jesus is the exalted King, but soon He will be the undisputed King. Paul is referring to the day Jesus returns. At the second coming no one will be able to deny that Jesus is in charge. Paul says, "every knee should bow . . . every tongue confess that Jesus Christ is Lord" (v. 10). This does not mean everyone will do so willingly. When Jesus returns, all those who trust Him for salvation will rejoice as we bend the knee in honor of our King. Those who reject Christ will also bend the knee, but they will do so unwillingly. Their hearts will not have turned to Him in faith, but they will be unable to resist His authority as King. How blessed it will be on that day to confess with joy Jesus is our Savior.

BONUS WEEK E
FOCUSING ON PHILIPPIANS 2:17–30

THERE IS NOTHING quite like a road trip to bring friends together. I (Chris) still laugh as I recall some of the shenanigans I engaged in with my college and seminary buddies. In fact, it was a road trip that led Katie and me to start dating.

It all started the year before my junior year of college. That summer I was on a missions trip across the United States. When I got back to school all I heard about was how much fun all my friends had back in Jacksonville, Florida, that summer. After being regaled by story after story of all I missed out on I decided I would stay in town the next summer and participate in every activity this group wanted to do.

If we fast forward to the next summer the first item on the docket was a trip to the lake in Alabama. At the time, Katie's parents had a lake house, which was the site of one of the previous summer's events. I was bound and determined to make the lake trip that year. As the time approached more people started backing out of the trip, but I was undeterred. The week leading up to the big trip there was only four people left: Katie, myself, and two other friends. Days before we were scheduled to leave the last two backed out.

Left with the choice of staying in Jacksonville or heading to the lake, I chose the lake. Katie and I left Jacksonville as just friends, but on the trip I started to want something more. I credit that road trip with bonding us in a way we previously had not been.

Paul experienced a similar bonding time with Timothy and Epaphroditus on his second missionary journey. These men formed a trust and companionship on this trip that would be recorded in the pages of Scripture.

As you study this passage, we pray God would give you friends like Paul found in Timothy and Epaphroditus. We pray God would send mentors into your life who will act as guides and coaches and that God would also give you opportunities to pour your life into others.

Foundation

Read and copy Philippians 2:17–30.

Observation

Note all you can learn about Timothy from these verses. Do the same for Epaphroditus. Note the command Paul gives to the church regarding these two men.

Clarification

- ▨ **DECIDE:** Look for potential key words in 2:17–30.
- ▨ **DISCOVER:** Choose a word to look up to find its original Greek word.
- ▨ **DEFINE:** Fill out a Greek study chart to learn more about that word.

Utilization

Follow the cross-references in this week's passage. Here are a few to start with:

to send Timothy (v. 19)

1 Corinthians 4:16–17

1 Thessalonians 3:1–3

as a son with a father (v. 22)

1 Timothy 1:2

2 Timothy 1:2

honor such men (v. 29)

1 Thessalonians 5:12–13

1 Timothy 5:17

Summation

- ▨ **IDENTIFY**—Find the main idea of this passage.
  Consult commentaries to double check your conclusions.
- ▨ **MODIFY**—Evaluate my beliefs in light of the main idea.

Do I regularly thank, recognize, and honor those who are serving to minister to me? Who am I pouring my life into?

■ **GLORIFY**—Align my life to reflect the truth of God's Word.
What is God leading me to do as a result of this week's study?

POINTS TO PONDER

Living as a Christian means we seek the good of others.

In verse 17 Paul says he is being poured out as a drink offering for this church. In the first century it was common to include sacrifice as a part of ritual worship. Some offerings had leftover meat, which could be sold at the market. A drink offering, however, was gone once poured out. You could not collect it again and reuse it. Paul is saying this is the way he is being spent for their sake. Paul's efforts for the cause of Christ have landed him in jail, and he is facing the real threat of death. He is assuring this church that if this is the case, it was worth it. He was willing to be used up so that they may come to know Christ and grow in Him. We too must be willing to be used up for the glory of God.

Living as a Christian means we rejoice always.

Paul continues his thought about being poured out as a drink offering by adding that he rejoices in this present suffering. Rejoicing is a consistent theme in Philippians. Paul rejoices in prison, that he is suffering, and that his life is being used up by God for others. If we knew our death was imminent, would rejoicing be the posture of our hearts? If Paul can rejoice in these circumstances he can rejoice in any, and so should we.

Find a Timothy.

In verse 19 Paul indicates his intent to send Timothy to Philippi to check on the church and bring back a report. Paul trusts Timothy greatly, calling him a son. Paul had no actual, familial relationship with Timothy but was his mentor. Paul did not try to do all the ministry by himself; he built a team to accompany him on his missionary journeys. Timothy was added before the second missionary journey and quickly became Paul's right-hand man.

If Paul, the most prolific missionary and New Testament author couldn't do the work all by himself, what makes us think we can do everything on our own? In whatever capacity you minister to others, make sure you are not trying to go it alone. Build a team and find people like Timothy who can be trusted to carry out valuable tasks.

Be a Timothy.

Think about the people you work with. Think about the people you serve alongside in your church. Would they describe you the way Paul describes Timothy? Are you trustworthy? Are you loyal? Do you have a Paul figure in your life who is mentoring you? We all need people like Timothy into whom we can pour our lives. We also need people like Paul who can pour into us. This is the pattern we see in 2 Timothy 2:2. Paul expected Timothy to take what he had learned from Paul and pour it into others who would do the same. If you have been blessed to have someone pour into you, don't let the chain be broken with you. Find others to disciple, and teach them how to disciple others.

Be willing to give up everything for the sake of Christ.

In verse 25 Paul introduces us to his other companion, Epaphroditus. Paul tells us that Epaphroditus is very sick and nearly died. Epaphroditus isn't suffering from indigestion; Paul says he risked his life for the mission. Epaphroditus seems to be on the mend by the time Paul writes this letter, but the precedent has been set.

The world is not impressed by tame, bland Christianity. The world was turned upside down when a band of first-century disciples decided they were willing to risk their lives to share the word. Epaphroditus, and others like him, remind us there is a fate worse than death.

Our health comes to us by God's mercy.

Though Epaphroditus was near death, Paul says, "God had mercy on him" (v. 27). It is easy to take our health for granted. It's always harder to recognize things that don't happen, rather than things that do happen. We recognize the near-miss car accident but don't recognize when God held us at a red light to keep us from a drunk driver down the road. Epaphroditus was willing to sacrifice his life and health because he knew God could heal him, and if God chose not to heal him the cause of Christ would still be worth the risk. If you are in good health today, stop and thank God for His mercy in your life.

Care for the sick among you.

Not only was God merciful to Epaphroditus, He was merciful to Paul. As a dear friend and fellow worker in the gospel, Epaphroditus's health weighed heavily on Paul's mind. Had anything happened to him Paul says he would have had, "sorrow upon sorrow." This language indicates that Paul cared deeply for this friend. We too should care for the sick among us. We need each other the most when we are at our most vulnerable. Do you know anyone who is sick today? Why don't you take a minute to pray for them? Pray that God would restore their health. Pray also that God would give you the same concern for others as Paul had for Epaphroditus.

BONUS WEEK F
FOCUSING ON PHILIPPIANS 3:1–6

HAVE YOU EVER been so mad that you yelled at the television? For me (Chris) this usually only happens if I'm watching my University of Florida Gators play football, and even then I'm relatively calm. I say *relatively* because I have been in the room with others who are much more vocal toward their television sets. Yes, I'm talking about Katie. When Katie watches her beloved Auburn Tigers she yells and cheers with reckless abandon. We are both known to get riled up about college football.

Others get equally riled up about politics. Elections provide plenty of fodder for many to get hostile with their televisions. People on both sides of the political spectrum have a lot to complain about, as do those who do not align themselves with either major party.

Still others get testy about music. They like what they like, and everything else is garbage. Some insist they don't make music like they used to, while others believe only the latest and greatest will suffice. Trying to engage in friendly debate with these audiophiles may lead you into dangerous territory.

Of course nothing quite compares to the hostility of one Wisconsin man in 2010. He got so upset over an episode of *Dancing with the Stars* that he shot his television with a shotgun. This led to a 15-hour standoff between the man and the police.

What we get riled up about says a lot about us. Paul gets riled up about the influence of false teachers in Philippi. In your study of the passage this week, try to figure out why Paul is so upset. Pray God would give you a righteous anger for the things that displease Him and the ability to let go of things that do not rise to this level.

Foundation

Read and copy Philippians 3:1–6.

Observation

Note all the commands Paul gives in this passage.

Look for all that Paul mentions could give him confidence in the flesh.

Clarification

- **DECIDE:** Look for potential key words in Philippians 3:1–6.
- **DISCOVER:** Choose a word to look up to find its original Greek word.
- **DEFINE:** Fill out a Greek study chart to learn more about that word.

Utilization

Follow the cross-references in this week's passage. Here are a few to start with:

we are the circumcision (v. 3)

Romans 2:29

Galatians 5:6

put no confidence in the flesh (v. 3)

Romans 15:17–18

Galatians 3:2–3

Galatians 6:14

whatever gain I had (v. 7)

Luke 14:27, 33

Summation

- **IDENTIFY**—Find the main idea of this passage.
  Consult commentaries to double check your conclusions.
- **MODIFY**—Evaluate my beliefs in light of the main idea.
  What is my confidence primarily in?
  Am I willing to count everything as loss so that I may have intimacy with Christ?
  What am I holding on to that is keeping me from a deeper relationship with Him?
- **GLORIFY**—Align my life to reflect the truth of God's Word.
  What is God leading me to do as a result of this week's study?

POINTS TO PONDER

Beware of false teachers.

In verse 2 Paul tells the church to look out for dogs. Philippi was not suffering from an infestation of feral canines, he was referring to false teachers. Specifically, the false teachers were those who sought to circumcise Gentile converts. It was their belief that in order to be a Christian, one must first convert to Judaism. This issue had already been decided by the Apostles (Acts 15) but this group, known as the circumcision party, has rejected this decision and is dead set on circumcising new converts. Paul calls them dogs because he detests their theology.

Christians can have sincere disagreements about some elements of doctrine (for example, the order of end-time events, mode of baptism, or governance structure of the local church). There are, however, some core components of the faith that, once removed, destroy the gospel altogether (for example, deity of Jesus, Christ as only way to salvation, or salvation by grace through faith).

This is what was happening in Philippi and was the reason Paul was so disturbed. This circumcision party was adding requirements to the gospel that should not exist. The gospel is not faith in Jesus plus our works. It is just faith in Jesus. We should take caution in whom we tag with the "false teacher" label. Again, we don't call everyone who doesn't agree with us on every point of theology a false teacher. This designation was reserved by Paul and others for those who altered the gospel.

Beware of those teachers who want to add requirements to the gospel. We cannot work for our salvation, and anyone who teaches otherwise is a false teacher.

Treasure Jesus above all else.

In verses 4–6, Paul talks about his religious accomplishments as a Jew. If you were creating a Pharisee all-star team, Paul would be on it. As Paul looks at these qualities he previously held and compared them to Christ, he calls them all rubbish. They were as useless to him as yesterday's garbage.

If you have ever been to a gym you have probably seen those people who love to look at themselves in the mirror as they work out. This narcissism is exactly what Paul wants us to avoid. Compared to the joy of knowing Christ, our accomplishments mean nothing. Be careful of falling in love with your work for the mission of God. The enemy would love nothing more than for you to focus on how much you do for God, rather than enjoy God's presence in your life.

BONUS WEEK G
FOCUSING ON PHILIPPIANS 3:12–16

A FEW YEARS ago we were in the process of moving from Jacksonville, Florida, to Atlanta, Georgia. We had the trip all planned out. Our convoy would roll out of Jacksonville first thing in the morning and arrive in Atlanta with several hours to spare. We would then sign the closing papers on the new house and spend the last few hours of daylight unloading the rental truck. You can probably guess that if all of that went as planned we wouldn't be writing about it now. No, almost none of those things happened.

Somewhere between Macon and Atlanta there was a fender bender that slowed down every lane and put us an hour behind schedule. This set off a chain reaction of delays that ultimately led us to being stuck in rush hour traffic. Downtown Atlanta at rush hour is not much fun in a car, but it is downright brutal in a 26-foot moving truck.

I (Chris) hate being stuck in traffic. Every fiber of my being is saying, "I'm not supposed to be here, I'm supposed to be up there!" Every moment sitting idle is a wasted moment, in my opinion. Every trip we take I know the amount of time it should take to get to our destination, and I am constantly comparing our progress to that ideal time. Frustration mounts when where we are and where we should be diverge.

I don't just feel that way on the road. I also feel this way when I'm walking. If I'm walking through a store and I can see people blocking the aisle ahead, I'll walk around several aisles until I find an unblocked lane. I don't want to wait on people to move, I don't want to break my stride; I don't want to stop moving forward.

If left unchecked this tendency could make me a colossal jerk when I'm driving or walking. The realization of this possibility is often enough to reign in the more sinister effects of my desire to move forward. However, it seems some of my preferences spring from a good place. I believe God gives us the desire to move forward in our spiritual life. If we are satisfied with complacency regarding our faith something has gone awry. This week we will look at this idea of moving forward.

As you study, we pray God would give you a holy discontent with stagnancy and a healthy desire to move forward.

Foundation

Read and copy Philippians 3:12–16

Observation

Note all the declarations Paul makes of his life's pursuits.

What is the ultimate goal of these pursuits?

Clarification

- **DECIDE:** Look for potential key words in Philippians 3:12–16.
- **DISCOVER:** Choose a word to look up to find its original Greek word.
- **DEFINE:** Fill out a Greek study chart to learn more about that word.

Utilization

Follow the cross-references in this week's passage. Here are a few to start with:

forgetting what lies behind (v. 13)

Luke 9:62

for the prize (v. 14)

1 Corinthians 9:24–25

call of God (v. 14)

Ephesians 4:1-6

2 Timothy 1:9

Hebrews 3:1

Summation

- **IDENTIFY**—Find the main idea of this passage.
  Consult commentaries to double check your conclusions.
- **MODIFY**—Evaluate my beliefs in light of the main idea.
  What is the goal of my life? What am I pursuing most of all?
  How do these pursuits line up with Paul's?

How am I running the race of faith?

*Not Moving, Holding
on to My Old Ways*

*Straining Forward to What Lies Ahead
with Determination and Daily Discipline*

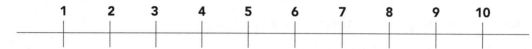

1   2   3   4   5   6   7   8   9   10

■ **GLORIFY**—Align my life to reflect the truth of God's Word.
What is God leading me to do as a result of this week's study?

POINTS TO PONDER

Know where you are.

If you are ever lost and need directions, maps can be extremely helpful. A map, though, is of no use if you don't know where you are to begin with. Paul starts this passage by admitting he knows exactly where he is. In verse 12 he says he has not yet attained his goal, nor is he perfect. This is the starting point of spiritual growth.

Faith grows in the soil of humility. It is only once we realize our imperfection in comparison with a holy God that we can know His mercy and grace. Further, we must admit, in humility, that we cannot overcome our sin problem on our own. Additionally, we must confess our need for Jesus daily if we hope to grow in faith. A proud heart says, "I have grown enough." A humble heart says, "I still have a long way to go."

In order to experience the type of growth Paul was chasing we must take the same posture he took, and conclude that we are not yet perfect. We must also come to believe that we will never enter perfection until we are in glory. It is this realization that there is much left to do that compels us to strive forward.

Forget the past (within reason).

Paul says he seeks to forget those things in the past. Here is where some of you will be thinking, "Those who neglect the past are bound to repeat it." Paul is not suggesting we find some sort of memory-erasing devise and completely forget anything other than the present. Remember the context of this statement. In verses 4–7 Paul was talking about his past accomplishments, his spiritual résumé. He is particularly in favor of forsaking past attempts to approach God on our terms. For Paul this meant he was trying to be the best Pharisee he could. For us this will probably looked a little different. Maybe we tried to win God's approval with good conduct or church attendance. Others may have sought God through an alternate religion. Still others may have assumed God was in favor of their sinful lifestyle since He never hit them with any lightning bolts.

Whatever your past spiritual failures may be, they are not the daily focus of those growing in Christ. If you are truly a believer, all of your sin is paid for: past, present, and future. It does no good to dwell on past sins, so leave them in the past. Don't let the enemy or anyone else accuse you of those sins. They are nailed to the Cross, and they define you no more.

Look to the future.

The second half of forgetting the past is looking to the future. In verses 13 and 14 Paul says he is "straining forward to what lies ahead. I press on toward the goal for the prize of the upward call of God in Christ Jesus." The past will always loom large if we are not intent on understanding the future. While we may not know every detail of how the end will come or what eternity will look like, we do know enough. We know that for those who love Christ there will be no punishment. Not only will God withhold the punishment we deserve, He will also give us rewards for our faithfulness. The ultimate reward for a Christian is being with God without an encumbrance of sin or brokenness. When we understand how great eternity will be, we will find it easier to let go of the past.

Stay on track.

In verse 16 Paul encourages the church at Philippi to, "hold true to what we have attained." Remember this letter contains no rebuke. Why then would Paul need to remind a relatively healthy church to hold true? Because getting off track is an ever present temptation for believers. We can be following Christ faithfully one day and find ourselves deep in sin the next. The whole idea of striving forward and looking toward the future requires we do these things continuously. No one applauds a derailed train for how long it stayed on the tracks. It could have successfully navigated thousands of miles, but if it becomes derailed minutes before its final destination the headline will always be about the derailment. Since it is possible to go off the rails at any moment, we should maintain vigilance at all times. Are there any areas that cause you to get off track? Are there any common pitfalls that divert your attention from Christ and what lies ahead? Pray that God would reveal these places to you so you can avoid them in the future.

BONUS WEEK H
FOCUSING ON PHILIPPIANS 3:17—4:3

FOR MANY YEARS Katie's family held a reunion in eastern Kentucky. The reunion was usually held at a state park that featured hiking trails, a large hotel, and a massive pool. One of the family traditions was heading down to Hoedown Island on Friday and Saturday nights. Hoedown Island is the proper name of an actual island located at the park. This patch of soil is just large enough to fit a concrete dance floor surrounded by metal bleachers. On most weekend nights you can find an old fashioned caller barking out signals on a PA system to square dancers who respond to every beck and call.

This haunt is mostly visited by the local community, with a smattering of tourists staying at the park hotel. The locals know by heart which songs are for square dancing and which are for line dancing. Since most of the out-of-towners don't know the difference between a promenade and a do-si-do, we sit out the square dances. However, when it comes to line dancing we laymen are more willing to give it a shot.

Square dancing requires precision. If you don't know what you are doing, you can throw everyone off. Line dancing, on the other hand, is a little friendlier to the boot-scooting novice. In line dancing the trick is to find someone who really looks like they know what they are doing, and copy them.

This is the sort of thing Paul is encouraging the Philippian church to do in their lives—copy him. Since many will seek to lead believers away from the faith, it is imperative that true disciples pattern their lives after other true disciples. Failure to do so leaves only one option—patterning your life after a fake disciple. Paul is not filled with conceit as he says this, rather, he is filled with concern.

As you study this week, we pray God will reveal to you the importance of having heroes in the faith—men and women you can look up to and model your life after.

Foundation

Read and copy Philippians 3:17—4:3.

Observation

Look for all the commands given in this passage.

Note all that is true of you as a Christian in verses 20–21.

Clarification

- ■ **DECIDE:** Look for potential key words in Philippians 3:17—4:3.
- ■ **DISCOVER:** Choose a word to look up to find its original Greek word.
- ■ **DEFINE:** Fill out a Greek study chart to learn more about that word.

Utilization

Follow the cross-references in this week's passage. Here are a few to start with:

our citizenship is in heaven (3:20)

Ephesians 1:18

Ephesians 2:19

stand firm (4:1)

1 Corinthians 15:1

1 Corinthians 16:13

Galatians 5:1

Summation

- ■ **IDENTIFY**—Find the main idea of this passage.
  Consult commentaries to double check your conclusions.

- ■ **MODIFY**—Evaluate my beliefs in light of the main idea.
  Do I view heaven as my true home? Do I long for heaven? Or am I too attached to the things of this world?
  What is my foundation? Am I standing on the truths of the gospel for my significance and purpose or what the world says I should be?

■ **GLORIFY**—Align my life to reflect the truth of God's Word.
What is God leading me to do as a result of this week's study?

POINTS TO PONDER

Real heroes live lives worthy of imitation.

It may seem quite egocentric for Paul to insist that this church follow his example. I would argue, though, that we are always setting examples for others to follow. Children will always be influenced by their parents. The parent can say, "Do as I say, not as I do," but children will always find it easier to replicate the actions of a parent rather than the intentions of that same parent.

Paul understands this church will always see him as an authority figure, a model they should pattern their lives on. Rather than reject this responsibility with an "aw shucks" false modesty, Paul welcomes the spotlight. We should welcome other Christians to follow the pattern of our lives. Hesitation in this respect is usually due to the fact that we have things we would like to keep hidden from others. Paul's life was an open book, and ours should be too.

Avoid harmful influence.

Paul returns to the idea of false teachers that he previously mentioned at the beginning of the third chapter. This time Paul gives the church some things to look out for when it comes to false teachers.

1. They lead you away from biblical Christianity. Paul says such people have destruction as their end, meaning their purpose is not to build up the church but to tear it down. Paul adds "their god is their belly" (v. 19). They do not actually worship the one true God, so following them will lead us further away from God. If a teacher is leading you away from the God of the Bible he or she is a false teacher.

2. They are characterized by indecency. In verse 19 Paul says these false teachers "glory in their shame." They take what is shameful and hold it up as commendable. If Scripture condemns an activity, we must condemn it too. Sure we can love those who struggle with condemnable sin patterns but we must never affirm or enable the sin. Teachers who applaud such indecency are not speaking the truth. They may believe their positions enable them to love sinners, but biblical love does not recategorize sin and call it worthy of honor. Real love warns people who are in danger, it cannot pretend danger doesn't exist.

3. They are unspiritual. Paul notes these false teachers' minds are set on earthly things. Those teachers whose minds are set on the earthly are they who seek to exploit others for material gain. The 1980s were rife with scandal as televangelists had moral failure after moral failure. These prominent preachers fell into sin chasing after money, sex, or both. The Bible clearly teaches that pastors who labor in teaching deserve to be provided for by their congregations (1 Timothy 5:17–18). This, however, is a far cry from gold-plated pulpits, $3,000 suits, and private jets. If a teacher is asking for your money but has no pastoral connection with you, they are most likely false teachers with their minds set on earthly things.

Be quick to reconcile with other Christians.

The one issue Paul addresses in this letter is a disagreement between two women in the church. Apparently this issue is major enough that Paul knows about it but not so divisive that he issues a rebuke. Paul speaks out of love for these two. He knows both of them and counts them as co-workers for the gospel. It hurts his heart that these two beloved sisters in Christ were divided. He asks the church to step in and help them agree in the Lord.

One of the inherent dangers of church life is we will have the opportunity to disagree. This is actually a good sign. Disagreements mean there are two parties that care enough about the church to have a divergent opinion. It also means people feel comfortable enough to voice alternate opinions without fear of reprisal.

Obviously, disagreements are not always healthy—things can go too far and healthy disagreement can quickly turn to toxic division. Our goal when disagreements arise in the church is not to get our own way or take our ball and go home. The goal is reconciliation. This is what Paul urges the church to help these women find. This is what we are to seek when the occasion arises.

BONUS WEEK I
PHILIPPIANS 4:10–14

HOW DO YOU know you are loved? This is a concept we cover with every couple in premarital counseling. One of the most helpful resources on this topic is Gary Chapman's *The 5 Love Languages*. Chapman believes everyone has a preferred method of giving and receiving love. He categorizes these love languages as physical touch, words of affirmation, quality time, gift giving, and acts of service. It is important to know how a loved one receives love. If your spouse receives love best through quality time, yet you continually attempt to demonstrate your love by giving gifts, you will find yourself frustrated . . . and broke!

Our youngest son Michael receives love through words of affirmation. Every time I (Chris) ask him how he knows I love him he says, "Because you've told me like a million times!" Though I'm sure this is an exaggeration, his point is well taken. I do tell him I love him often because I don't want him to ever question whether or not he is loved.

In the same way your heavenly Father does not want you to question whether or not He loves you; the answer is an emphatic, "Yes!" One of the ways we know He loves us is that He sent Jesus to the world to die on the Cross for our sin. Another way He demonstrates His love for us is by His provision. How many meals have you skipped? How many nights have you spent without a roof over your head? Perhaps the most common way God demonstrates His love for us is through answering prayer.

We often approach the Lord in prayer in the pit of despair and experience His goodness as we feel our fears allayed and worries calmed. Since God is both loving and powerful He cares about the things that concern us and is capable of acting on our behalf.

As you study our passage this week, notice how much God loves you. Note also how our view of God affects our experience of Him. We pray He will give you a proper perspective of Him and your troubles.

Foundation

Read and copy Philippians 4:10–14.

Observation

List all the circumstances Paul has found himself in.

Note what he says he's learned from these experiences.

Clarification

- ▩ **DECIDE:** Look for potential key words in Philippians 4:10–14.
- ▩ **DISCOVER:** Choose a word to look up to find its original Greek word
- ▩ **DEFINE:** Fill out a Greek study chart to learn more about that word.

Utilization

Follow the cross-references in this week's passage. Here are a few to with:

through Him who strengthens me (v. 13)

Romans 16:25

2 Corinthians 12:9–10

Ephesians 3:14–21

1 Timothy 1:12

Summation

- ▩ **IDENTIFY**—Find the main idea of this passage.
  Consult commentaries to double check your conclusions.

- ▩ **MODIFY**—Evaluate my beliefs in light of the main idea.
  Can I say that I can be content with plenty and hunger, abundance and need?
  How do my previous thoughts about the popular coffee cup and T-shirt verse, "I can do all things through him who strengthens me," compare to what Paul meant by this statement?

- ▩ **GLORIFY**—Align my life to reflect the truth of God's Word.
  What is God leading me to do as a result of this week's study?

POINTS TO PONDER

Find contentment in God's provision.

One of the most popular Bible verses these days is Philippians 4:13. Did you notice in your study this week the context of this verse? Though we usually see this verse interpreted as a promise for God's help to accomplish difficult tasks, the proper context for this statement is Paul's discovery of contentment. He says he figured out how to deal with times of abundance and times of need by trusting God to provide. When we understand that all we have is from God, we can be confident that He will provide all we need. Once we have this assurance we can endure any circumstance.

It is interesting Paul says he needs God to strengthen him both when he is in abundance and need. It is easy to see why we need God's provision when we are in need, but why when we have plenty? Living in abundance often gives us a false confidence that we supply our own needs. Paul understands that especially in times of plenty we need God to set us free from slavery to possessions. Whether we have much or little we are called to trust God's provision. Doing so produces contentment that can weather all seasons.

BONUS WEEK J
PHILIPPIANS 4:15–23

WHEN KATIE AND I were first married we worked with Cru (then known as Campus Crusade for Christ). Cru has no central funding through which to pay its employees, so we had to raise our own support to be able to minister on college campuses. While Katie excelled at this task, I always found it difficult to ask people for money.

Cru had a great little software program that helped keep track of donors, pledges, and actual receipts. When you first launched the program it had one of the week's verses plastered on the screen. "And my God will supply every need of yours according to his riches in glory in Christ Jesus" (Philippians 4:19). This verse will always remind me of evenings I spent on the phone and the hours I spent in front of the computer screen tracking all the relevant data.

I'm glad this verse was incorporated into the design of that software because there were many occasions when we didn't know where the support would come from, or if it would come at all. In those moments all we could do was trust God would in fact provide for all our needs. Whether it was an extra gift from an existing partner or a random check from someone we hadn't spoken to in years, it seemed like God always showed up in our moment of need.

As you study our passage this week, notice Paul's confidence in God's character. He is convinced God will give him all he needs. Even if Paul has a need that goes unmet, he knows God will give him the ability to go without. Additionally, Paul is also convinced God will provide all of the needs for the church of Philippi.

As you begin your study time this week, we ask God would give you the same confidence as Paul. We also pray God would remind you of His provision, so you may not take any of it for granted. Finally, we pray God would meet every need you have this week.

Foundation

Read and copy Philippians 4:15–23.

Observation

Note all Paul teaches on giving. List out all that is true about God in these verses.

Clarification

- **DECIDE:** Look for potential key words in Philippians 4:15–23.
- **DISCOVER:** Choose a word to look up to find its original Greek word.
- **DEFINE:** Fill out a Greek study chart to learn more about that word.

Utilization

Follow the cross-references in this week's passage. Here are a few to start with:

the fruit that increases to your credit (v. 17)

2 Corinthians 5:9–10

Ephesians 6:6–8

a sacrifice acceptable and pleasing to God (v. 18)

Micah 6:7–8

Romans 12:1

Hebrews 13:16

Summation

- **IDENTIFY**—Find the main idea of this passage.
  Consult commentaries to double check your conclusions.
- **MODIFY**—Evaluate my beliefs in light of the main idea.
  Am I a partner with those in ministry? Do I pray for them and give to their needs? Are the deeds of my life characterized as a fragrant offering? Do I believe God will supply every one of my needs?
- **GLORIFY**—Align my life to reflect the truth of God's Word.

  What is God leading me to do as a result of this week's study?

POINTS TO PONDER

Partner with others as an overflow of your contentment.

In Philippians 4:14–16 Paul talks about the richness of the partnership he enjoys with this church. Apparently they partnered with him financially when no other church would. Paul used the funds they gave him to further his ministry and the cause of Christ. Paul never forgot their generosity and partnership.

One of the ways we demonstrate contentment with God's provision is sharing generously with others. Specifically, we are called to give to kingdom causes that help the gospel go forth. While there is nothing inherently wrong with giving money to cancer research or community organizations, the church has the responsibility to take the gospel to the nations. Since we can't do this alone we must partner with other churches and agencies to maximize our efforts. Look for ways to invest in kingdom work. Start with your church. Give a percentage of your income to your local church. Beyond that find organizations that are doing good work with groups that are close to your heart.

Biblical giving is not about the money, it's about the heart.

In verse 17 Paul clearly explains his motivation for asking for their partnership. Paul is no prosperity preacher; he asks because he is convinced the cause is worth it. Additionally, he believes that through giving this church will draw nearer to God. By giving up their money the church at Philippi was able to demonstrate their contentment in God's provision and their trust that He will continue to supply their needs.

Many people complain that churches and pastors just want their money, but most pastors care more about your soul than your giving record. If you love your money more than you love God, this is an indication you don't truly trust Him. By giving generously to your church and other kingdom causes you indicate there is something more precious to you than money.

Contentment comes from trusting God's character.

In verse 19 Paul tells us why he is so confident that God will provide for this church. He says God provides "according to His riches." A promise to provide is only as good as the wealth of the one making the pledge. During a telethon anyone can call and pledge $10 million. This pledge is worthless, though, if you don't have that money to give. Paul's confidence rests in the fact that God is able to fund every endeavor He sets out to fund. Since we know God is able to provide and we trust His character we have nothing to worry about.

APPENDIX

OVERVIEW OF PHILIPPIANS

Author

IN VERSE 1, Paul identifies himself as the author of this epistle to the Philippians. Paul also identifies Timothy as his companion but not necessarily his coauthor. While some people question the authenticity of Paul's authorship of this and other works, we believe the Bible is trustworthy in its claim of Pauline authorship.

Readers of the New Testament first meet Paul in Acts 7. This chapter relates the story of Stephen, a deacon in the Jerusalem church (6:5), his testimony before a religious council (7:1–53), and his death by stoning (vv. 54–60). Paul, who was called Saul at the time, stood watch over the garments of the rock throwers as they pelted Stephen to death (v. 58). In the next scene Paul is actively persecuting Christians for their faith (8:1–3). Acts 9 tells of Paul's encounter with Jesus. While traveling to Damascus to persecute more Christians, Paul experienced a blinding light, along with the voice of Jesus (vv. 1–19). Convinced of Jesus' authority, Paul commited to follow Christ.

Paul became a prominent figure in the church at Antioch (13:1). While serving in this church the Lord commissioned Paul and his friend Barnabas to a missionary journey (13:2). Paul would embark on three such journeys (chapters 13, 15, and 18). On these journeys Paul preached in synagogues to announce to the Jews that the Messiah had come. Once people responded in faith, Paul organized them into churches. Paul would stay as long as he could with these churches but eventually moved from town to town throughout the Mediterranean. On some occasions, Paul would only have a matter of weeks in a city, as in Thessalonica (17:1–9). On other occasions, Paul could stay longer, as with in Corinth (18:1–17).

A major shift happened in Paul's ministry when he heard the "Macedonian Call." The Holy Spirit did not allow Paul to minister in the territory of Asia (16:6). At that time Asia was not the continent we know but a province in Asia Minor. Instead, Paul received a vision from God to go to Macedonia (vv. 9–10). The city of Philippi was a prominent town in Macedonia.

Timeline of Paul's Life

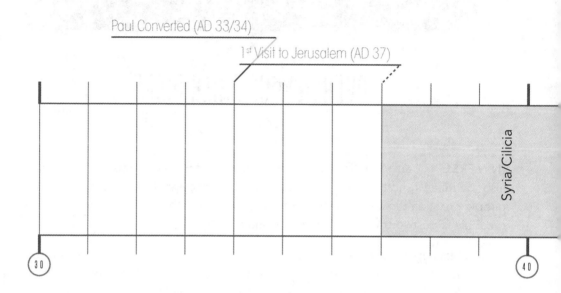

Paul Converted (AD 33/34)

1st Visit to Jerusalem (AD 37)

Syria/Cilicia

30

40

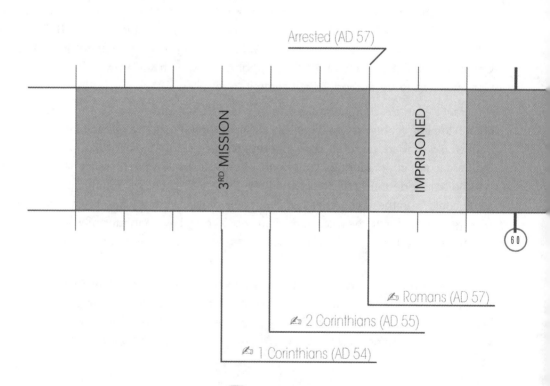

Arrested (AD 57)

3RD MISSION

IMPRISONED

60

Romans (AD 57)

2 Corinthians (AD 55)

1 Corinthians (AD 54)

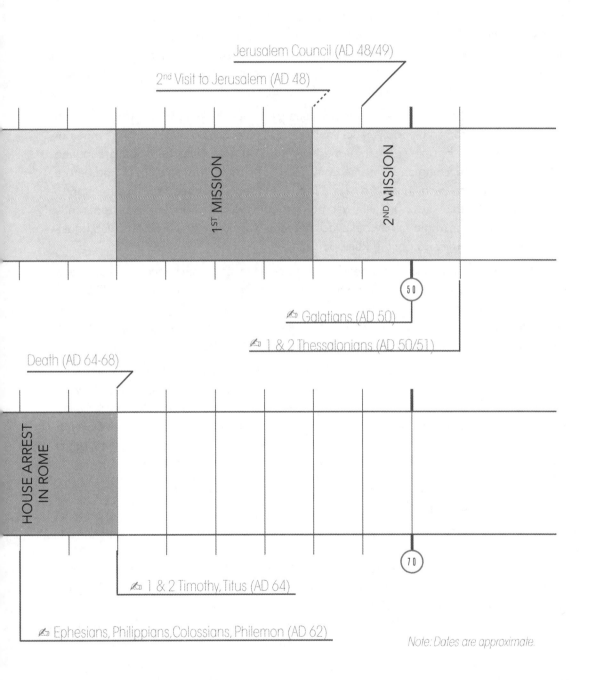

Jerusalem Council (AD 48/49)

2nd Visit to Jerusalem (AD 48)

1ST MISSION

2ND MISSION

50

✎ Galatians (AD 50)

✎ 1 & 2 Thessalonians (AD 50/51)

Death (AD 64-68)

HOUSE ARREST IN ROME

70

✎ 1 & 2 Timothy, Titus (AD 64)

✎ Ephesians, Philippians, Colossians, Philemon (AD 62)

Note: Dates are approximate.

Audience

Philippi was a Roman colony in Paul's day (Acts 16:12) named after Philip II, the father of Alexander the Great. Philippi had been previously occupied by Greeks, Macedonians, and then it was taken over by the Romans. Battles in the area following the death of Julius Caesar brought large numbers of soldiers. When these armies achieved victory they were disbanded and many veterans stayed to colonize Philippi.

Luke reports that during his second missionary journey, Paul came from Troas, through Samothrace, then on to Neapolis, and finally on to Philippi. Upon arrival, Paul's missionary cohort meets a businesswoman named Lydia (v. 14). Lydia was part of a group who listened to Paul's teaching and became convinced of its truth. She worshiped God before Paul's party came to town, and Luke says, "The Lord opened her heart to pay attention to what was said by Paul" (v. 14). Lydia was the first convert in Philippi and was apparently very influential—her whole family believed after she was converted (v. 15). Lydia's house became the missionary outpost in Philippi.

One day, Paul and Silas were headed to a prayer meeting and encountered a slave girl. This girl was possessed by a demon, which gave her fortune-telling abilities. The slave girl made a pattern of following Paul and his companions and calling out their identities and purposes. Out of annoyance, Paul commanded the spirit to leave the girl, and it did (vv. 16–18). The girl lost her fortune-telling powers, which greatly upset her owners.

This event led to the persecution of Paul and Silas. These men were beaten and imprisoned. In the middle of the night Paul and Silas are released from prison by an earthquake, which broke their bonds. When the missionaries didn't leave immediately they were able to console the suicidal jailer and lead him and his family to faith. Daylight brought the realization that Paul and Silas were Roman citizens. As citizens, their rights had been violated, which caused the local magistrates great fear (vv. 22–38).

Paul also visited Philippi on his third missionary journey, but not much is known about his time there on this trip (20:1–6).

Aim

Paul wrote this letter from prison (Philippians 1:7). Typically, Paul's letters—also known as epistles—follow the same format: greeting, acknowledgement of what the church is doing right, followed by a rebuke for what the church is doing wrong. Philippians does not contain a formal rebuke. This epistle is the most encouraging of all of Paul's writings. Genuine affection flows from Paul's pen as he writes to this beloved church.

Many themes are prominent throughout the letter: encouragement (1:3–11), assurance of God's sovereignty (vv. 12–14), importance of the gospel (vv. 15–18), living for

Christ without fear (vv. 19–26), holiness (vv. 27–30), unity through humility (2:1–11), our part and God's part in sanctification (vv. 12–18), partnership in ministry (vv. 19–30), righteousness comes by faith (3:1–11), perseverance (3:12—4:1), reconciliation in the church (4:2–3), role of prayer and thought-life (vv. 4–9), and contentment (vv. 10–20).

Like most books in the New Testament there is some debate about the date Paul wrote the letter. Twice Paul mentions some details about his current surroundings that help date the epistle. In 1:13, Paul mentions the Imperial Guard. This is a military unit assigned to guard the Roman emperor. In 4:22, Paul sends greetings from those in "Caesar's household." It is likely Paul is in contact with these groups because he is in Rome awaiting trial. If these two references are indications that Paul was in Rome awaiting trial, the letter would date between 60–62 AD, as this was the time he was known to be there.

Outline

As you study, fill out the chart below with a title that summarizes each potion of Scripture.

1:1–2

1:3–5

1:6–11

1:12–18

1:19–26

1:27–30

2:1–8

2:9–11

2:12–18

2:19–30

3:1–6

3:7–11

3:12–16

3:17–21

4:1–3

4:4–9

4:10–14

4:15–20

4:21–23

GLOSSARY OF BIBLE STUDY TERMS

- **Interlinear Bible:** a translation where each English word is linked to its original Greek word. There are many free interlinear Bibles online, as well as great apps you can download to your phone or tablet. Check out KatieOrr.me/Resources for current links.

- **Concordance:** a helpful list of words found in the original languages of the Bible (mainly Hebrew and Greek) and the verses where you can find them.

- **Cross-reference:** a notation in a Bible verse that indicates there are other passages that contain similar material.

- **Footnote:** a numerical notation that refers readers to the bottom of a page for additional information.

- **Commentary:** a reference book written by experts that explains the Bible. A good commentary will give you historical background and language information that may not be obvious from the passage.

- **Greek:** the language in which most of the New Testament was written.

- **Hebrew:** the language in which most of the Old Testament was written.

STRUCTURE AND BOOKS OF THE BIBLE

Old Testament

⇉ Books of the Law (also known as the Pentateuch)

Genesis	Numbers
Exodus	Deuteronomy
Leviticus	

⇉ Books of History

Joshua	2 Kings
Judges	1 Chronicles
Ruth	2 Chronicles
1 Samuel	Ezra
2 Samuel	Nehemiah
1 Kings	Esther

⇉ Wisdom Literature

Job	Ecclesiastes
Psalms	Song of Songs
Proverbs	

⇉ Major Prophets

Isaiah	Ezekiel
Jeremiah	Daniel
Lamentations	

⇉ Minor Prophets

Hosea	Nahum
Joel	Habakkuk
Amos	Zephaniah
Obadiah	Haggai
Jonah	Zechariah
Micah	Malachi

New Testament

» **Narratives (First four together are known as "The Gospels")**

Matthew

Mark

Luke

John

Acts

» **Epistles (or Letters) by Paul**

Romans

1 Corinthians

2 Corinthians

Galatians

Ephesians

Philippians

Colossians

1 Thessalonians

2 Thessalonians

1 Timothy

2 Timothy

Titus

Philemon

» **General Epistles (Letters not by Paul)**

Hebrews

James

1 Peter

2 Peter

1 John

2 John

3 John

Jude

» **Apocalyptic Writing**

Revelation

MAJOR THEMES OF THE BIBLE

Though many view Scripture as a patchwork of historical accounts, morality tales, and wisdom for daily living, the Bible is really only one story—the mind-blowing story of God's plan to rescue fallen humanity. This storyline flows through every single book, chapter, verse, and word of Scripture. It's crucial that we know the movements, or themes, of the grand storyline so we don't miss the point of the passage we are studying.

For example, I grew up hearing the story of David's adulterous affair with the beautiful, but married, Bathsheba. I heard how he covered his misdeeds with a murderous plot to snuff out her husband. This story was usually punctuated with a moral that went something like this, "Don't take what isn't yours!" While it is indeed good practice to refrain from taking what isn't ours, there is a much bigger connection to the grand story that we will miss if we stop at a moral lesson. So what then is this grand story, and how can we recognize it?

The story falls into four main themes, or movements: creation, fall, redemption, and completion*.

Creation

The Bible begins by describing the creative work of God. His masterwork and crowning achievement was the creation of people. God put the first couple, Adam and Eve, in absolute paradise and gave them everything they needed to thrive. The best part of this place, the Garden of Eden, was that God walked among His people. They knew Him and were known by Him. The Bible even says they walked around naked because they had no concept of shame or guilt. (See Genesis 2:25.) Life was perfect, just like God had designed.

Fall

In the Garden, God provided everything for Adam and Eve. But He also gave them instructions for how to live and established boundaries for their protection. Eventually, the first family decided to cross a boundary and break the one rule God commanded them to keep. This decision was the most fateful error in history. At that precise moment, paradise was lost. The connection that people experienced with God vanished. Adam and Eve's act was not simply a mistake but outright rebellion against the sovereign Creator of the universe. It was, in no uncertain terms, a declaration of war against God. Every aspect of creation was fractured in that moment. Because of their choice, Adam and Eve introduced death and disease to the world, but more importantly, put a chasm between mankind and God that neither Adam nor Eve nor any person could ever hope to cross. Ever since the fall, all people are born with a tendency to sin. Like moths to a light, we are drawn to sin, and like Adam and Eve, our sin pushes us further away from any hope of experiencing God. You see God cannot be good if He doesn't punish sin, but if we all receive the punishment our sin deserves we would all be cast away from Him forever.

*For a more detailed discussion on these themes, refer to Part 1 and 2 of The Explicit Gospel by Matt Chandler (pages 21–175) or Chapter 2 of Mark Dever's The Gospel and Personal Evangelism (pages 31–44).

Redemption

Fortunately, God was not caught off guard when Adam and Eve rebelled. God knew they would and had a plan in place to fix what they had broken. This plan meant sending Jesus to earth. Even though Jesus was the rightful King of all creation, He came to earth in perfect humility. He walked the earth for more than thirty years experiencing everything you and I do. Jesus grew tired at the end of a long day. He got hungry when He didn't eat. He felt the pain of losing loved ones and the disappointment of betrayal from friends. He went through life like we do with one massive exception—He never sinned. Jesus never disobeyed God, not even once. Because He was without sin, He was the only one in history who could bridge the gap between God and us. However, redemption came at a steep price. Jesus was nailed to a wooden cross and left to die a criminal's death. While He hung on the Cross, God put the full weight of our sin upon Jesus. When the King of the universe died, He paid the penalty for our sin. God poured out His righteous anger toward our sin on the sinless One. After Jesus died, He was buried and many believed all hope was lost. However, Jesus did not stay dead—having defeated sin on the Cross, He was raised from death and is alive today!

Completion

The final theme in the grand storyline of the Bible is completion, the end of the story. Now that Jesus has paid the penalty for our sin, we have hope of reconciliation with God. This is such tremendous news because reconciliation means we are forgiven of sin and given eternal life. Reconciliation means God dwells with us again. Finally, we know Him and are known by Him. Completion for us means entering into reconciliation with God through the only means He provided. We can only experience reconciliation under God's rescue plan if we trust Jesus to pay for our sin and demonstrate this by repenting, or turning away, from our sin. But God's rescue plan does not end with us. One day, Jesus will come back and ultimately fix every part of fallen creation. King Jesus will come back to rule over God's people, and again establish a paradise that is free from the effects of sin.

Let's return to the David and Bathsheba story for a moment and try to find our place. David was the greatest, most godly king in the history of the Old Testament, but even he was affected by the fall and had a sinful nature. This story points out that what we really need is not a more disciplined eye but a total transformation. We need to be delivered from the effects of the fall. It also illustrates how we don't simply need a king who loves God, but we need a King who is God. Do you see how this story connects to the arc of the grand storyline? Just look at how much glorious truth we miss out on if we stop short at "don't take what isn't yours."

HOW TO DO A GREEK/HEBREW WORD STUDY

Learning more about the language used in the original version of Scripture can be a helpful tool toward a better understanding of the author's original meaning and intention in writing. The Old Testament was written in Hebrew and the New Testament in Greek. Though the thought of learning a new language is overwhelming to most of us, we live in an age with incredible tools at our fingertips through smartphone apps and online websites (many of which are free!) that make understanding the original meaning as simple as looking a word up in a dictionary.

Here are three easy steps to work toward a better understanding of the verses you study.

DECIDE which word you would like to study.

Do a quick read of your passage and note any potential keywords and/or repeated words. There is no right or wrong way to do this! Simply select a few words you would like to learn more about.

DISCOVER that word as it was originally written.

Using an interlinear Bible (see glossary), find the original Greek (if New Testament) or Hebrew (if Old Testament) word for each instance of the word in the passage you are studying. There may be more than one Greek or Hebrew word present that translated into one English word.

DEFINE that word.

Look up your Greek/Hebrew word (or words if you found more than one) in a Greek/Hebrew lexicon. Most of the free apps and websites available do this with a simple click of a button, opening up a wealth of information referenced from a lexicon they've chosen. I encourage you to check out the videos I've created to show you how to use many of the online Greek tools. You can find them at KatieOrr.me/Resources.

Though this step can seem overwhelming, once you find an app or site you love, it is as simple as looking up a word in the dictionary. Here is a chart you can use to record what you learn.

Greek/Hebrew Word Study Worksheet

GREEK WORD: VERSE AND VERSION:

Part of Speech:
(verb, noun, etc.)

Translation Notes:
(How else is it translated? How often is this word used?)

Strong's Concordance Number:

Definition:

Notes:

HOW TO DO A GREEK/HEBREW WORD STUDY—EXAMPLE

Let's walk through this process, looking at Hebrews 11:1 together. I've also included extra notes to help you better understand the behind-the-scenes work the apps and websites are doing for us.

DECIDE which word you would like to study.

Since Hebrews is in the New Testament, we'll be working with the Greek language. To start your Greek study, look for any potential keywords in Hebrews 11:1. As you find any repeated word or words that seem important to the passage, write them down.

faith, assurance, hoped, conviction, things, seen

Since faith is probably what the main point of this verse is about, let's study this word together.

DISCOVER that word as it was originally written.

Now that we know what we want to study, we can look up the English word *faith* in an interlinear Bible to find out what the original Greek word is. An interlinear Bible will show you English verses and line up each word next to the Greek words they were translated from. If you own or have seen a parallel Bible, with two or more English translation versions (ie, ESV, KJV, NIV) lined up next to each other, this is the same concept. Interlinear Bibles have the original language alongside an English translation.

Let's take the first phrase in Hebrews 11:1 to see how this works:

Now faith is the assurance of things hoped for. —Hebrews 11:1

In Greek, it looks like this: *ἔστιν δὲ πίστις ἐλπιζομένων.*

Most people (including me!) can't read this, so the transliteration of the Greek is often provided for us as well. This transliteration is simply the sound of each Greek letter turned into English letters to spell out how the Greek is read. It's a phonetic spelling of the Greek word. For example, the first Greek words we see, *ἔστιν* and *δὲ*, are transliterated into *estin* and *de*, which is how they are pronounced.

The interlinear Bible simply lines up the two versions (and typically the transliteration as well) so we can see which word goes with which, like this:

ἔστιν	δὲ	πίστις	ἐλπιζομένων
estin	de	pistis	elpizomenōn
is	now	faith	of things hoped for

Now you can use this layout to find the original word for faith. Do you see it?

Faith=pistis=πίστις

DEFINE that word.

Now that we know the original word for faith used in Hebrews 11:1 is *pistis*, we can look up that Greek word in a Greek lexicon (which is like a dictionary) and note what we learn about the original meaning of the word. I've provided a worksheet to record this info. *(For a free printable version of this worksheet, go to KatieOrr.me /Resources and look for the PRINTABLES section.)*

GREEK WORD:
pistis

VERSE AND VERSION:
Hebrews 11:1

Part of Speech: (verb, noun, etc.)	Translation Notes: (How else is it translated? How often is this word used?)
noun	used 243 times in the New Testament ESV. All but two times it is translated "faith." Other two translations: assurance (1) and belief (1)

Strong's Concordance Number: G4102	Definition: faith, confidence, fidelity, guarantee, loyalty

Notes:

pistis, which derives from **peithomai** ("be persuaded, have confidence, obey"), connotes persuasion, conviction, and commitment, and always implies confidence, which is expressed in human relationships as fidelity, trust, assurance, oath, proof, guarantee. Only this richness of meaning can account for the faith (**pistei, kata pistin, dia pisteos**) that inspired the conduct of the great Israelite ancestors of Hebrews 11.

THE GOOD NEWS

God Loves You

You are known and deeply loved by a great, glorious, and personal God. This God hand-formed you for a purpose (Ephesians 2:10), He has called you by name (Isaiah 43:1), and you are of great worth to Him (Luke 12:6–7).

We Have a Sin Problem

We are all sinners and are all therefore separated from God (Romans 3:23; 6:23). Even the "smallest" of sins is a great offense to God. He is a righteous judge who will not be in the presence of sin and cannot allow sin to go unpunished. Our natural tendency toward sin has left us in desperate need of rescue because God must deal with our sin.

Jesus Is the Only Solution

Since God's standard is perfection, and we have all fallen short of the mark, Jesus is the only answer to our sin problem (John 14:6). Jesus lived a life of perfect obedience to God. So when Jesus died on the Cross, He alone was able to pay the penalty of our sin.

After His death, Jesus rose from the dead, defeating death, and providing the one way we could be reconciled to God (2 Corinthians 5:17–21). Jesus Christ is the only one who can save us from our sins.

We Must Choose to Believe

Trusting Christ is our only part in the gospel. Specifically, the Bible requires us to have faith in what Christ has done on our behalf (Ephesians 2:8–9). This type of faith is not just belief in God. Many people grow up believing God exists but never enter into the Christian faith. Faith that saves comes from a desperate heart. A heart that longs for Jesus—the only solution for their sin problem—to be first and foremost in their life. We demonstrate that we have this type of saving faith by turning away, or repenting, from our sin.

FOCUSED15 STUDY METHOD

Apply this method to two to ten verses a day, over a week's time, for a deep encounter with God through His Word, in as little as 15 minutes a day.

Foundation: Enjoy Every Word

Read and rewrite the passage—summarize, draw pictures, diagram sentences, or simply copy the passage. Do whatever helps you slow down and enjoy each word.

Observation: Look at the Details

Take notes on what you see—write down truths in this passage. Look for truths about the character of God, promises to cling to, or commands given.

Clarification: Uncover the Original Meaning

- **Decide which word you would like to study.**
  Look for any repeated words or keywords to look up, choose one, and learn more about it.
- **Discover that word as it was originally written.**
  Using an interlinear Bible, find the original Greek or Hebrew word for the English word you chose.
- **Define that word.**
  Learn the full meaning of the word using a Greek or Hebrew lexicon, which is very much like a dictionary.

Utilization: Discover the Connections

Cross-reference—Look up the references in each verse to view the threads and themes throughout the Bible.

Summation: Respond to God's Word

- **Identify—Find the main idea of the passage.**
- **Modify—Evaluate my beliefs in light of the main idea.**
- **Glorify—Align my life to reflect the truth of God's Word.**